Brian Macdonald

# *Wildlife Diary*

## A Year in the Old Welsh County of Meirionnydd

ILLUSTRATIONS BY C. F. TUNNICLIFFE O.B.E., R.A.

*Wildlife Wales* 2016

First published 2016
Copyright © Brian Macdonald
Illustrations by permission of the Tunnicliffe Estate
ISBN 978-1-5262-0565-0
www.wildlife-wales.co.uk
Designed and produced for Wildlife Wales by Uniformbooks
Distributed by the Welsh Book Council
Printed in Great Britain by TJ International Ltd, Padstow, Cornwall

# *Introduction*

THE FOLLOWING weekly wildlife diary entries were originally written for a local newspaper. All are based on observations made within five miles of Llanbedr situated just inland of the north end of Cardigan Bay, the long coastline that sweeps up from Pembrokeshire northwards to the Llyn Peninsula. This beautiful location includes the Rhinog Mountains: moorland and lakes with spate rivers feeding into the River Artro that runs down through a wooded valley, through Llanbedr to the estuary, exiting into Tremadog Bay at Llandanwg: a great variety of rich habitat and outstanding landscapes.

Writing this diary was an enriching experience involving as it did recalling memorable moments of the previous week and finding the words to convey with clarity some heart-lifting images and experiences; not least, the challenge of reducing an embarrassment of riches to the 300 words required by the newspaper.

Almost as much pleasure was gleaned from searching through a collection of books illustrated by the inimitable C. F. Tunnicliffe O.B.E., R.A. for images to suit each entry.

First coming to public attention just before the last war as the illustrator of *Tarka the Otter* by Henry Williamson, Tunnicliffe illustrated many books produced throughout the same war, apparently for maintaining morale and a love of country through difficult times. *The Seasons and the Gardener* beautifully written for children by H. E. Bates was the first of many Tunnicliffe illustrated books collected over many years, found in second-hand book shops thoughout the UK.

Tunnicliffe himself moved to Wales with his wife just after the war ended, setting up home and studio at Malltraeth on the Cefni Estuary on the south-west coast of Anglesey where he lived for the rest of his life as described in his *Shorelands Summer Diary*. In all, Tunnicliffe illustrated about 300 books, as well as many individual studies and pictures, many of which can be seen today in the Oriel Ynys Môn in Anglesey. The Tunnicliffe Estate has kindly allowed the reproduction of many of his illustrations for the purpose of this *Wildlife Diary*.

Gerard Manley Hopkins, who also enjoyed this area, wrote the following in his famous poem, The Windhover:

> "*My heart in hiding*
> *Stirred for a bird,—the achieve of, the mastery of the thing!*"

It is hoped that this collection of diary entries of observations made in this wonderful area of Wales along with C. F. Tunnicliffe's illustrations conveys at least some of the joy of the original memorable moments to the reader.

BRIAN MACDONALD

# Wildlife Wales

THE RHINOG MOUNTAIN range comprises some of the most remote and wild landscape in the country: peaks of 2500ft enclosing valleys and lakes each with its own unique character, spate rivers cascading down valley and ravines, through moorland, woods and rough pasture to the estuary and sea. This variety of landscape provides habitat for a great range of plants and wildlife. *Wildlife Wales* exists to help visitors and residents alike to appreciate and enjoy this rich environment.

www.wildlife-wales.co.uk

# Wildlife Diary 2007

### JANUARY
| | |
|---|---|
| *New Year* | 11 |
| *Winter Gales* | 12 |
| *First Stirring of Spring* | 13 |
| *Dunlin* | 14 |

### FEBRUARY
| | |
|---|---|
| *Conspicuous Shelduck* | 15 |
| *Winter* | 16 |
| *Jack Snipe* | 17 |
| *Spring Foraging* | 18 |

### MARCH
| | |
|---|---|
| *Frogs* | 19 |
| *Spring Progress* | 20 |
| *Chiffchaff Arrival* | 21 |
| *Frog Legs* | 22 |
| *Blackcap Sub-song* | 23 |

### APRIL
| | |
|---|---|
| *Eider* | 24 |
| *Migrant Arrivals* | 25 |
| *Trees* | 26 |
| *Welcome Rainfall* | 27 |

### MAY
| | |
|---|---|
| *Swifts* | 28 |
| *Foxgloves & Campion* | 29 |
| *Smell of Rain* | 30 |
| *Insect Eaters* | 31 |
| *May Morning* | 32 |

### JUNE
| | |
|---|---|
| *Wildlife Walk* | 33 |
| *Boat Trip* | 34 |
| *Llyn y Feddw* | 35 |
| *Moth Catching Notes* | 36 |

### JULY
| | |
|---|---|
| *Duneland Summer* | 37 |
| *Summer Foraging* | 38 |
| *Bright & Fresh* | 39 |
| *Summer Rain* | 40 |

### AUGUST
| | |
|---|---|
| *Turn of the Year* | 41 |
| *Lilliput* | 42 |
| *Rockpooling* | 43 |
| *Chanterelles* | 44 |
| *Whimbrel* | 45 |

### SEPTEMBER
| | |
|---|---|
| *September Fly-fishing* | 46 |
| *The Great Ash* | 47 |
| *Early Autumn* | 48 |
| *Peregrine* | 49 |

### OCTOBER
| | |
|---|---|
| *Merlin* | 50 |
| *Departures & Arrivals* | 51 |
| *Dolphins* | 52 |
| *Late Season Bass* | 53 |

### NOVEMBER
| | |
|---|---|
| *Autumn Woodland* | 54 |
| *High Rhinogs* | 55 |
| *Tracks* | 56 |
| *Winter Light* | 57 |
| *Grayling* | 58 |

### DECEMBER
| | |
|---|---|
| *December Gales* | 59 |
| *Winter Gulls* | 60 |
| *Winter Frost* | 61 |
| *Memorable Images* | 62 |

NOTES ON THE TEXT
Names of organisms in italics are featured in the glossary of English Welsh Taxonomic names p.63. The exception to this rule is the naming of moths which was largely a Victorian innovation with no Welsh tradition except for the commonest species.

# New Year .................................................. 4th January

SOME MEMORABLE SIGHTINGS over the Christmas period despite return of winter gales: walking the bridge at Porthmadog, cap low in stinging rain, a small, neat gull caught the eye not 20 yards away, repeatedly lifting up in the stiff westerly and dropping down on the harbour waters below: distinctive, sooty band behind the head and wide, silver wing like *Common Gull*, only lacking black and white tips. A *Black-Headed Gull* arrived with fine, white and silver wings and sooty spot behind the eye, conveniently confirming the small size. The now anticipated dark underside to the wing was occasionally visible from the high vantage point. Winter sightings of *Little Gulls* are becoming more frequent, especially between Porthmadog and Pwllheli, the western seaboard offering milder winter conditions than continental breeding areas; a fine, unexpected bonus to a grim afternoon in town.

Before New Year, whilst advancing carefully across the salting to view roosting *Teal* and *Wigeon* on the estuary, *Teal* calls and sudden movement revealed a dark, compact form, low and fast over the water, straight towards us. Lifting to clear the bank, a pale and orange-brown underside flared as a small, male *Merlin* stalled and banked sharply away to speed north along the salting edge and away over the dyke.

Later, walking downstream, something odd caught the eye: a dark branch appeared static in the receding tide, low in the pale water, mid-section submerged. Binoculars revealed nostrils, whiskers and eyes at water level looking directly at us, tail behind. The large, dog *Otter* moved quietly past upstream not 40 yards away, like a large eel on the surface, still visible as it slipped under the wavelets. We left him, still moving unhurried upstream, to find *Otter* prints in the sand, five pads spread wide, sand too hard to take the web.

# *Winter Gales* .................................................................... 11th January

IF SUMMER IS REMEMBERED for lack of rain, this winter will be memorable for gales. Despite overnight storm and rain and creamy seas, sky clears blue, and the wind, though strong, is warm.

*Gulls* hang on the updraft from dunes; *Ravens* patrol low along the same windward dune face. Occasional small *Finches* and *Meadow Pipits* braving the gale are gusted back inland, too windblown for clear identification, calls lost in rush of wind.

*Teal* and *Wigeon* shelter under the near shore, careful approach giving close views before panic sets in. *Redshank* flight away tight and low; lipstick-red legs and bills and startling white wing bars illuminate soft grey plumage.

Nearing the shore, parties of *Wigeon* and *Teal* move off at intervals, struggling low against wind and wave, when a powerful, heavy, slate-blue form looms behind.

Without effort, the *Peregrine* prospects the little flock below for fools or weaklings before allowing the wind to power a return upstream. Up it beats again against the gale, starting up another small *Wigeon* party from the waves. Without height to power a stoop and too close to water to risk a miss, strong duck are safe, but the *Peregrine* above  dominates with power and command, easily breasting and oblivious to tumultuous winds as the black-hooded head turns to inspect the flock below, yellow legs tucked neatly under stubby tail. Half hope my vertical form, telescope and tripod might be taken for a useful observation post when once again the wind powers a wide banking turn, swinging away across the salting.

Later, whilst scanning shore and raging seas, the same dark, powerful, sickle-winged form clips the circular, black-framed binocular view, which followed confirms the fastest moving life form on earth; parties of escaping *Oystercatcher*, *Knot* and *Curlew* beat low over creamy surf in its wake.

# *First Stirring of Spring* .................. 18th January

WE ARE VERY LUCKY: spring lasts from January to June. Snowdrops, *Cyclamen coum* and *Crocus tommasinianus* are flowering in the gardens and the dawn chorus gathers momentum daily, easily heard these dark mornings. Whilst changing for work behind closed curtains, *Robin* and *Song Thrush* song rings out across the village in the half light, a *Great Tit* chimes out its two notes in the woods, a party of *Siskins* sails over the trees with wheezy calls and a pair of *Bullfinches* pipe quietly in the apple trees.

Prolonged gales have reduced the range of birds at the Maes even on quiet days: *Thrushes, Finches, Chats* and *Buntings* have shifted to sheltered inland feeding. *Black Scoter* are visible on wave crests, with the odd *Diver* showing pale or in flight over the sea. Westerly gales not only make viewing difficult, but seabirds find sheltered feeding in the lee of the Llyn, the other side of Tremadog Bayay. The estuary holds the usual suspects: *Wigeon* flight out to sea and back to graze according to tide; *Teal* sleep or preen on shining mud; *Redshank* numbers have increased as they retreat from exposed shores. Good to find a female *Goldeneye* quietly feeding in flat water, eponymous golden eye clear in a deep maroon head over white streaked, soft grey, back.

Interested to find *Porphyra umbiliculis* abundant with bladder wrack, like shiny green-black, wet bat wings plastered over round boulders. Appearance not too appetising, but tastes nutritious and sustaining like fresh, steamed kale. Packed with protein, iodine and many vitamins, taste does not belie its worth, as is appreciated in the Gower where laver is a local speciality. Look forward to inflicting on the family, perhaps quickly steamed with cumin and eaten with fresh, crusty bread or to complement roast lamb and creamed potato.

# *Dunlin* ............................................................. 25th January

GOOD, BITING, MORNING FROST today; bright sun in deep blue sky later. No need for a coat for the first time in weeks. Flight calls now audible so species count increases accordingly. Two *Skylarks* creeping through the mown grass of the camp field on Saturday feed in the same spot, joined by a third, four days later. A new flock of 50 *Dunlin* stream up the estuary to sweep and alight among *Teal* feeding in shallow water over mud. *Wigeon* graze hard behind on the salting.

Later, on the shore, the same *Dunlin* sweep back and forth along the strand, undersides shining white over dark seas as the flock turns and wheels searching for quiet feeding. Interesting to watch the dynamics of the flock: moving as a single organism fast and low over the waves; slowing to alight then off to wheel about and scan again along boulder strewn shore.

Though less elegant, fast and precise, similar dynamics may perhaps be seen in the mass movement of a football crowd; however, to watch precisely synchronised fast flickering wings over the sea slowing to equally synchronous intermittent flick and glide low over the shore is wonderful and incomprehensible.

Of interest and possible clue to understanding came when the landward wing of this particular flight took an independent decision to alight and remain on shore, the seaward majority turning away again, perfectly united in their continued indecision.

The eight remaining *Dunlin* proved a delight: watchful whilst allowing careful approach to within six paces, binoculars now superfluous. Each slow pace, in time with the gentle waves, caused muted trills and a few running steps of the closest birds: no panic or flight; all clearly *Dunlin* with black legs and watchful black eyes; each subtly different in black bill length and warm, scaled plumage.

# Conspicuous Shelduck ............................ 1st February

IN THE FIRST GREY LIGHT of dawn, the air resounds with Thrush song, five to eight birds immediately surrounding the house with unaccountably more in the background; early enough to mingle with *Tawny Owl* calls in the oak wood.

On the Maes, *Skylarks* still feed on the same small area of mown campsite. Whether the insectivorous diet previously assumed or winter addition of seeds and shoots later found to be the case, for 10 m2 of turf to sustain 2-3 birds for a week is surprising.

Numbers of *Mallard* and *Shelduck* increase by the week in the estuary: three *Mallard* were observed flying in from the mountains; *Shelduck* numbers are in the twenties. The evolutionary logic that produced such beautiful, striking, and boldly marked plumage is beyond understanding: pure white with black flashed wings, wide chestnut breast band, mallard-green neck and head, and deep red bill. In  some birds, female preference has pushed male plumage to impractical and dangerous excess, but female *Shelduck* lack only the swan-like red bill knob of the males. Perhaps *Shelduck* meat is so unpalatable that predators are discouraged, giving freedom to evolve the striking plumage so common on our estuaries.

The much smaller *Ringed Plover* have similarly bold, banded markings on white plumage, but the small flock that swept over the beach before us effectively disappeared on alighting amongst pebbles. Magical to locate them with the telescope: diminutive, with sand brown backs, all facing the same way; all boldly ringed and masked black on white; only the occasional late or young bird less boldly banded.

As we left the beach, a female *Goosander* occasionally surfaced in only inches of water right on the tide line, streamlined form so similar to the shallow wavelets that, though close by, it was hard to locate and point out.

# *Winter* ......................................................................... 8th February

SNOW FALLS STEADILY this afternoon. A biting, early morning, east wind whipped snow from the fields, misting out the dog trotting ahead. Yesterday's frost remained white all day in shade, sorrel leaves frozen when gathered late afternoon. Ivy quivers, alive with *Pigeons*, *Blackbirds* and *Thrushes* feasting on funereal fruit; metallic pink ivy seeds litter the ground as the fruits ripen.

Tuesday, still and bright: *Woodpecker* drums a mile distant over the estuary; air-bubbles heard from shallows, forced from tide pressed sand. *Wigeon*, *Teal* and *Gulls*, silhouetted on the tide-filled lagoon, stream out on the outgoing current feeding hard, *Redshank* and *Oystercatchers* on the salting behind.

On the breakwater, the light is perfect to find silver-grey *Knot*, warm-packed amongst tide-wet boulders. Larger, scattered, black and white *Oystercatchers*, feed, preen or sleep. Telescope reveals, first one, then many diminutive *Ringed Plover* almost indistinguishable in dry boulders above the tide mark.

*Turnstones* feed busily, mottled, bladderwrack-brown, moving in and out of view, short orange legs occasionally bright on

dark weed. Three grey *Dunlin* perch alert on high boulders. Long, low waves break peacefully along the shore. Drake *Merganser*, all showy white, black and red, streams out fast on the outflow behind.

Suddenly, piping wader calls resound and sunlit white bellies flare out against dark waves as flocks wheel and turn in panic.

A scan of the boulders reveals a superb, amber-gold *Merlin*, upright on a high rock, glaring about, recovering from a failed sortie. Soaring reconnaissance; dive for momentum; streak behind the breakwater; flip over for surprise: a tactic often used by *Merlin* and *Sparrowhawks*.

The *Merlin* leans forward, checks for *Ringed Plover*, then flicks back over the breakwater to retrace its flight path close by, alighting atop the yacht club stanchion before whipping low up the estuary for another chance to kill.

# Jack Snipe ............................................................... 15th February

OUT ON THE SALTING, the greensward is mazed with mud-bottomed creeks draining the highest tides back into estuary and dyke. *Wigeon* graze in a tight pack; *Curlew* stand preening or asleep on the grass, or with heads only visible above the salting whilst prospecting creeks with long, decurved bills. Rushes mark poorly drained land where *Meadow Pipits* and occasional *Reed Buntings* forage.

Fine, tan mud lays flat in the creek bottoms; a great variety of tracks and prints record the passing of birds and animals between tides. Whilst pouring wet plaster to record *Curlew* tracks, wings whirr as the dog flushes a *Snipe* from rushes close behind. *Common Snipe* zig-zag fast to the horizon, squelching calls like boots in wet mud. This bird flits quietly over the salting on down-curved wings to alight in rushes 40 yards distant. Marking the spot and plaster cast set, we set out to quarter the area to flush the bird for a better look.

The fact that this proved a lengthy business even with the dog is characteristic of a particular species. Another sudden whirr of wings from a muddy pool and the bird again flits over the salting to land in a shallow declivity in the estuary bank, this time clear of rush cover. Prints marked with a stick, a quiet approach gave a rare chance to observe a secretive bird out in the open.

At four yards, a buff striped, high crown is just visible in the cleft, beady eye below, when the dog moves out of heel and the bird springs the third time.

Lack of skylark-like white fringe to the trailing edge and noticeably shorter bill than common snipe confirms provisional *Jack Snipe* identification as this dainty bird alights again in a salting creek, this time safe across the estuary.

# *Spring Foraging* .................................................. 22nd February

WE ARE MOVING DAILY through the wide spectrum of spring that spans January to June. Just now, *Cornelian Cherry* (*Cornus mas*) acid yellow-green flowers cluster tight on bare twigs; first flowers of both wild white and cultivated pink forms of *Cherry Plum* (*Prunus cerasifera*) open like first stars at nightfall; *Forsythia* sprays a cheerful yellow; Acacia dealbata clouds powder yellow on fine, grey foliage.

*Blackbird's* mellow notes are now heard with the *Song Thrush* chorus, and a *Skylark* has started its cascade of notes over the Maes, evocative of summer days in open country. Last summer, one *Skylark* regularly hovered over the dunes, unable to sing, all liquid notes missing, leaving only unmusical trills. Maybe a voice defect or behavioural variation, or perhaps deafness: most songbirds instinctively make a basic effort to sing but need to compete and learn from neighbouring birds to develop a full song.

Now is a good time to be thinking about wild food, with fresh, green, spring growth shooting everywhere and shell-fish well in season. Last week, we gathered *Winter Purslane* (*Claytonia perfoliata*), *Corn Salad* (*Valeriana locusta*), and *Bittercress* (*Cardamine hirsuta*) for salad from one location and *Sorrel* (*Rumex acetosa*) from one field corner that grows leaves of size worthwhile for an excellent soup: good with a spoonful of yoghurt or fried cubes of bacon and bread. Fresh Mussels are tasty in white wine or smoked, whilst we recently found Winkles very worthwhile steamed in apple juice with an onion base. Looking forward to trying fried *Cockles* with laver bread, all gathered locally. Trout and Salmon are out of season in rivers and lakes, but we enjoyed *Grayling* last week for supper, though the time, cost and 'carbon footprint' of driving to the Dee may disqualify this wild winter sporting fish as truly 'wild food'.

# *Frogs* .................................................................................................. 1st March

EQUIPPED WITH WELLIES, aquaria and great enthusiasm, the fortnightly kids' group spread across the boggy meadow looking for frogspawn. Within minutes, sharp young eyes spotted a frog in the clear water of the drainage ditch, moving slowly over the bottom. The gathering group noticed more frogs, then many male frogs clasped in a great ball of clammy passion on the ditch floor, presumably attracted by an unfortunate female now at the core. Understanding gradually spread through the group, questions of the curious answered matter-of-factly by the worldly. Even these voices were a little hushed as we began to notice skins of frogs, some twitching underwater in ghostly fashion as small fish fed from the remains.

Spawn was soon found, a mass of jelly bubbled across the puddle surface; great tactile satisfaction in handling the elusive jelly stream, only a minimum for each tank to avoid overcrowding. *Water-Crowsfoot* and *Pondweed* offsets distributed for aeration and tadpole food, flat rocks found as islands for emerging froglets, and all was set with half a session remaining.

After looking for *Snipe* and discussing preparation and use of rushes as tapers, we looked at catkins of *Birch*, *Alder* and *Hazel*, claret tufts of *Hazel* flowers protruding from fruit buds to catch yellow catkin powder. Attention inevitably returned to the ball of *Frogs* still moving on the ditch floor. A *Birch* stem was used to gently float the ball to the surface. *Frogs* remained spraddled in cold passion, only a few dropping off en route, dispersing only when placed on a mossy rock, frogs plopping into the water below or hopping and crawling into the marsh. We later found a small pond with a better balance of sexes, frogs coupling everywhere; even some strings of *Toad* spawn suspended like telephone wires through the pondweed fronds.

# *Spring Progress* .................................................................. 8th March

ANOTHER FRESH, SPRING DAY, with black tadpoles wriggling and ivy-leaved crowfoot in delicate white flower in the tank on the landing windowsill. At the very tip of a *Cherry Plum* pink with blossom, a pale brown and buff *Song Thrush* belts resounding couplets into early morning blue sky.

On the estuary, all but four of two hundred over-wintering *Wigeon* and two out of one hundred *Teal* have departed for breeding locations, mostly further north. We shall miss the tight packs grazing on the salting; whistles and yelps and high skeins of sharp winged forms flighting over the dunes to the sea. Newly resplendent, burnt orange, *Great Crested Grebes* have left the bay for inland waters.

At the same time, *Redshank* are near the hundred mark, numbers swelled with passage birds, occasional *Godwits* and *Greenshank* also moving through. *Mallard* have returned, with about twenty *Shelduck* busy in the margins; and *Ringed Plover* are beginning to pair along the pebbled shore.

Inland, *Redwings* are restless as they move and flight though the tree tops, their fine whistled flight call heard again at night as flocks move north. *Woodpeckers* have been drumming for several weeks on fine, still mornings; this morning both *Green Woodpecker's* ringing note and harsh scolding of *Great Spotted Woodpecker* were heard from the same spot.

Though a few over-winter, returning *Chiffchaff* will soon be heard in the woods, with *Sand Martins* hawking for insects over water any day now, first sightings early in the month in the south.

Last night, house lights attracted many bone-white, dark specked, *Oak Beauty* moths to the windows, jostling plump bodied behind the glass. A joy to see first *Plum* blossoms just opening this evening, milk white on lower branch tips; glad the *Bullfinches* have not quite cleared the buds, despite winter morning raids.

# *Chiffchaff Arrival* ......................................................... 15th March

LAST YEAR, first *Chiffchaff* was heard here in the woods 1st April, after a cold month with snow. This year, three first sang on the beautiful morning of 13th March. Though increasing numbers are found here over winter, recoveries of ringed birds breeding in Ireland and Britain suggest that most over-winter south of the Sahara in Senegal, with passage recoveries all up the western Atlantic seaboard between. To hear the first of the year is a great seasonal landmark, simple two notes a backdrop to most days of spring and early summer.

A *Yellowhammer* started in wheezy refrain in gorse the beginning of March this year, much earlier than previously appreciated.

Yesterday, in the lane, first blue *Violets* nodded amongst glossy yellow, wide-open *Celandine* spokes in warm sun with grey-blue *Speedwell*. *Sycamore* buds burst in spectacular, slow explosion: salmon pink-sheened missiles split by inexorable expansion of pleated young leaves within, glossy reddish-green with vigour.

On the Maes, *Winter Purslane* gathered as salad a few weeks ago flowers: tiny, delicate white set in bright green leaf collar; an early naturalised introduction from the US pacific coast, first noticed 1852. *Stonechats* have paired, often together on fence tops, and the *Skylark* that cannot sing has returned, gamely buzzing tunelessly overhead. *Ringed Plover* chase and display over sand and water uttering haunting calls in strange, up-winged flight.

Interesting to see if dumpy little *Shags*, now sporting summer quiffs, will depart for cliff ledge nesting on the Llyn. One green-black, iridescent bird was washed up at the weekend, lower bill and throat appearing road-mark aerosol-sprayed, such thick, deep yellow marking. The same day saw *Stoat* scamper along slate bridge parapet to disappear in cracks, big *Hare* preoccupied with something interesting in rushes, and blunt-headed *Porpoise* barrelling in wave troughs beyond a *Shag* off shore.

# *Frog Legs* ......................................................... 22nd March

THE PAGES OF SPRING keep turning: clusters of tight, white *Blackthorn* buds finely massed on dark shoots; *Great Crested Grebes* enacting ages-old courtship rituals offshore, bill to narrow bill, pointing left and right on sinuous white necks then nodding by turn identical, burnt orange, crested heads.

Surprising to find a tight flock of 20 *Turnstones* speeding low over the waves; most wintering waders and duck are dispersed, though 20 *Mergansers*, clearly paired, also have yet to leave the estuary and shore and *Red-throated Divers* still show pale fronts amongst hundreds of black *Scoter* scattered across the bay.

Inland, a gothic frog tale continues to unfold before wide-eyed children signed up for the Wildlife Wales Kids' Group. On a recent excursion to collect frogspawn, an obvious imbalance of the sexes was leading to the demise of hard-pressed female frogs. Last weekend, for the benefit of new members, we diverted to a farm pond with a previously well-balanced population of *Frogs* and *Toads*.

This time, those first at the pond were obviously excited by something, shouting back and pointing. It transpired that pond and bank were littered with dead and dying frogs, all with hind legs bitten off entirely. *Herons* feed at the pond, but long bills, though ideal for spearing and stabbing, are not adapted to bite and chew. Likely predators would be able to swim and to be of sufficient size to hold the frogs whilst making one or two bites, hence *Otter* or *Mink*.

Further research has revealed two similar recorded incidents, one in the Grampians in April 2004, the other in Exmoor April 2002. Though not definitive, *Otter* was identified by the environment agency as the most likely predator that has learned to avoid toxic skins by removing the legs and skinning them to relish the meat within.

# *Blackcap Sub-song* ............................................................ 29th March

LAST YEAR *Blackcaps* were first heard in this woodland 4th April, only two days after arrival of the first *Chiffchaffs*. This year, the latter arrived over two weeks earlier on 13th March, so wonderful, liquid *Blackcap* notes are expected any day as they advertise their presence and stake territorial claims.

Passing beneath a plumose cypress bough on a beautiful spring Sunday morning a week or so ago, a long string of murmured notes streamed down to the path below. After careful watching, no movement was located in the dense, sun-warmed cypress, though the subdued liquid sub-song continued.

A stone gently lobbed into the thick fronds halted the song and a small bird flitted unobtrusively over the path into a less dense holly before resuming the gentle warble, as if to itself.

It still took a while of careful watching from different vantage points before a small movement revealed first a beady black eye, then soot-black cap and smoke grey plumage, perfect camouflage for deep shade under an umbrella of holly.

Especially as no full song has been heard since, it is probable that the bird described over-wintered, as do an increasing number of *Blackcaps* and *Chiffchaffs*, the warm spring day prompting a quiet song rehearsal before competitors arrive.

Last year, *Swallows*, *Wheatear* and *Sandwich Terns* were first seen 1st April, so are expected in the next few days, along with earlier *Sand Martins* and *Blackcaps*. Meanwhile, delicate stars of pure white *Greater Stitchwort* or 'daddies-shirt-buttons' opened on warm lane sides last week as the earlier *Celandines* begin to fade.

This year we tapped a *Sycamore*, a maple grown in these islands from Roman times, to boil down as syrup; over 6 litres of sap was piped into a plastic water container in 5 days before the hole was firmly plugged.

# *Eider* ............................................................................................ 5th April

STRANGE, UNSETTLING WINDS this spring: Sunday morning was quiet and bright on our seaward facing slope, but hard to run against a cold, dry, east wind on the ridge behind, mountains sunlit with a dry haze, more like dusty late summer. Wind now swung north with crystal clear atmosphere, but still dry and cold out of the sun.

Of awaited migrants, only *Wheatears* have arrived on the Maes, an area of salting and rabbit-cropped grazing behind the dunes; still looking for *Martins*, *Swallows* and *Blackcaps*

Today, nine *Eider* lay line astern off the headland and many seabirds of the rocky Llyn are feeding on this sandy side of the bay. *Razorbills* have been in evidence in  past weeks but today saw a lone *Gannet* in strong, long-winged flight high over the sea and *Manx Shearwaters* skimming the dark blue wavelets, splashing down to feed with mixed packs of shearwaters and gulls. *Shearwaters* were close to this shore last Easter, too, presumably following seasonal fish movements in the bay.

This morning, an early *Salmon* or *Sea Trout* leapt high and silver, splashing back into blue sea between two gulls just off shore. The margins of the estuary lagoon shimmer and hiss with the panic of six-inch, slim, silver-grey fishes, visible as long shadows on the sandy bottom.

In the woods, *Sorrel* is in delicate white flower over bright green shamrock leaves. 6 litres of *Sycamore* sap yields only a cream jug of syrup; great for roasting ham but only really worthwhile as an experiment.

A *Polecat* killed on the road below prompts a revised perception of current status. Advancing from previous isolated strongholds in dune systems on the west wales coast, this species is now found as far east as the Wales borders, another successful comeback for a past 'vermin' species.

# *Migrant Arrivals* .................................................. 12th April

WINDS HAVE SHIFTED west at last, but only a light drizzle to date and the river down at rocky bottom. Hope *Dipper* and *Wren* nests under bridges have survived bank holiday and low water. The bay was busy with pleasure boats and jet-skis for a couple of days before *Scoter*, *Divers* and *Shearwaters* could return. Packs of *Manx Shearwater* skim the seas on long, thin, black wings like small albatross, splashing down to feed together with gulls, *divers* and auks; mostly the blacker *Razorbill* with a few brown-black *Guillemot* identifiable with finer bills.

First *Terns* hawked high on fine white wings just off-shore over sun-glared sea, bleating harsh calls, folding into darts firing down into the sea below for small silver fish. Last year, *Sandwich Terns* returned first and remained most common through the year. Difficult to be sure without binoculars, but these birds seem smaller and lighter, so may be *Common Tern* or *Arctic Terns*.

Evocative *Willow Warbler* song with distinctive plaintive end trill was again first heard on high ground above the woodland where *Chiffchaffs* have been calling their signature two notes for weeks. Everything else is returning about 10 days later than 2006, though spring flowers are on cue. Pure white *Wood Anemone* spokes with boss of yellow stamens open in light shade over fine-cut foliage, seasonal landmark of early April.

The latest migrants are all spotted incidentally: first *Swallow* in classic needle-tailed pose on a telephone wire; snatches of *Garden Warbler* song heard from the bedroom; *Ring Ouzel's* wild notes from a rocky cwm in Cwm Nantcol. An exceptionally late winter *Fieldfare* called, 'swch, swch, swch', high in treetops before flying out westwards, still calling. The next morning brought first *Redstart* halting song, not easy to spot in a treetop over the path, even without leaves.

# *Trees* ........................................................... 19th April

ANOTHER PAGE of this wonderful spring unfolds as apples and pears come into blossom. Old *Pear* specimens tower next to farm cottages or bush against walls as outgrown espaliers, a slight creaminess to white massed blossom, with a hint of fresh leaf green unfurling. Ornamental *Crabs* in deep reds and pinks flaring out in gardens cannot compare with the delicate blush white of hedgerow crab or larger apple blossom. *Bees* move pollen between domestic and wild *Apples*, seedling trees in autumn showing the full range of resultant variation, from tiny, yellow, wild crabs, through red tinted fruit, to medium sized apples on seedling trees close to habitation.

Many florist flowers have graced our dining room in past weeks, but nothing has given more pleasure than a single *Sycamore* shoot, cut with glossy salmon pink buds almost 2" long that split and furl back as tight packed leaves force their way into light. Fresh, new green with a hint of red vigour, silvered with light down unpleats against the window pane, venation clear through translucent green, with tiny, green grape flower buds tight bunched at the base.

Flowers of many native trees emerge likewise with the leaves. *Oaks* are a bronze green amalgam of emerging new leaf and catkin, soon turning clear green as catkins wither, only to take on a red anthrocyanin hue of a second spurt of 'lammas growth' in summer, named after the Celtic festival of first fruits on 1st August. In autumn, the leaves turn various shades of yellow and brown, as chlorophyll is withdrawn from them and carotenoid pigments become visible instead.

A magnificent *Ash* with a girth greater than any listed for the UK stands alone in sheep cropped pasture; we still await the bursting of tight, purple grape flowers from matt-black, bishop's mitre buds.

# *Welcome Rainfall* ......................... 26th April

RAIN HAS CLEANSED THE AIR and filled the river, now in spate after weeks of drought.

Introducing young children to spring flowers took 30 minutes to progress 50 yards of lane: *Dandelion, Daisy, Ramsons, Plantain, Celandine, Primrose, Bluebell, Speedwell, Violet. Ivy-leaved Toadflax* quivered as something moved along the wall behind; a *Lizard* not sufficiently sun-warmed to escape. Released on a wide step before skittering to dark crack refuge; copper sheen of fine stippled brass over dark hide and fine, long toes splayed over warm slate.

Satisfying to see dark rain clouds streaming into the hills from the sea, bright sun lighting the landscape between.

A single valley yields two new migrants: *Whitethroat* rattling in *Blackthorn* scrub and *Grasshopper Warbler's* churring monotone from undrained fields beyond. A *Whitethroat* flipped up in halting song flight from the dunes this morning, one of many migrants landed in scrubby briar and bramble overnight to feed up for a day or two before moving to more familiar habitat. A *Sedge Warbler* scratched away close by; many minutes before a slight movement gave away a distinctive, eye-striped head, deep in briars. Worth the wait for an unexpected, female *Redstart* sighting, briefly visible just twice in the briar, red-brown tail spread in short flight.

Four *Dunlin* on the beach in various stages of black-bellied, rufous coated, summer plumage, a fifth bird, still grey and white, quickly moved up to feed on soft, dry sand. Black bill longer than *Dunlin*; preliminary identification of *Curlew Sandpiper* confirmed as pale rump showed in flight.

Next day two curlew-like birds moved off with a slightly smaller, grey wader. First guess at two *Curlew* with *Whimbrel* was adjusted on closer view: pale eye stripe and stouter bill turned the '*Curlew*' into *Whimbrel*; flight confirming smaller, grey and white *Bar-tailed Godwit*.

# Swifts ............................................................................................ 3rd May

ANOTHER HOT DAY down at the Maes: lots of hawthorn flies in the air, jet-black, legs trailing. A passer-by asked what was of interest so we chatted by the farm gate, scanning the landscape and listening for new species. Tops of fence posts, telegraph poles, wires, small trees and bushes are all productive visual focal points in a wide panorama, birds in flight picked up in the spaces.

This morning, agitated *Pied Wagtails* snapped attention to purposeful flight and glide of a *Sparrowhawk*, untroubled by the commotion. Later, scanning the skyline for raptors, first two *Swifts* of the year raced and stalled, hawking for flies high in the heat haze.

On the Maes, another *Sedge Warbler* scratched away, skulking in an island of bramble in rabbit-grazed turf. In the dunes behind, a *Whitethroat* flipped up in full song flight from an elder top, each new flight to a closer perch. Flitting across to the bramble top, it filled the telescopic field, white throat distended in rattling song, grey crest up; a superb composition with tan brown flight feathers.

*Sandwich Terns* hawked over green-blue, tide-filled lagoon: pure, angel white in buoyant, lilting flight; needle pointed wings and tail streamers closing into deadly darts. Jetting into the water with white, wind-blown spray, most emerge with sand eels held cross-wise in jet-black bills. A party rested on a wet sand bar, lifting and nodding black-crested heads, bleating strange, dry calls in display.

Last week, two *Whimbrels* were found on the beach, en-route between coastal African winter quarters and summer breeding in the Arctic Circle. Today, a flock of fifteen are hidden in boulders. Time to mark again: curlew-like but distinctive 'pi, pi, pi, pi, pi' flight call; size comparable to nearby *Oystercatcher*; bills short as young *Curlew* and flight light as a falcon.

# *Foxgloves & Campion* .................................................. 10th May

WEST WINDS HAVE RETURNED, cloud from the sea turning to rain over mountains: not enough to fill the river but reassuring to see the lawn green up. Most migrants are now arrived and busy with courtship and nesting; only a few straggling *Wheatears* still on the Maes, not yet left for mountain dry-stone walls.

The next run of still, warm evenings will be worth the trip to hear *Nightjars*, always a magical experience: never certain, always much later and darker than remembered. Ears, strained to hear soft 'churring' deep in bracken and heath, are tuned to the last sounds of a summer evening: late *Song Thrush*; early *Barn Owl*; *Oystercatchers* fussing in the estuary below; *Common Sandpiper* pair piping to each other.

Eventually, when moon and stars are out and even a breeze is an impediment to hearing, a soft, continuous, almost mechanical monotone 'churring' detaches itself from background sounds, fading and returning with the breeze or turn of the head. If lucky, a dark form flips and flaps in erratic flight between bush tops or low overhead with a soft 'quick, quick' call, clapping long wings overhead in display or threat, fine wing marking just visible in the dusk.

In lanes and woods, fragrant *Bluebell* and starry *Stitchwort* are still going strong with delicate *Woodruff* in patches of shade. The first wave of spring flowers—*Celandines* and *Primroses*—are now faded: just a few *Violets* remaining; white *Ramsons* thinning to green seeds. In their place, summer *Red Campion* has been in cerise pink flower for a couple of weeks now with *Foxgloves* towering up, first grey-pink buds showing purple flower tips. In the dunes, a patch of tough South African red-hot-poker has been in flower for a fortnight, not out of place in dry sand and sun.

# *Smell of Rain* .................................................................................. 17th May

RAIN STREAMED DOWN last night, the river roaring through the village this morning; little early for *Sewin*, though last evening one fish did swirl twice after the fly on the pool surface. May is fragrant as sweet azalea and lilac take over from fading wisteria; musky scents of *Hawthorn* and *Rowan* in the hedgerow hang in humid air with the smell of rain. *Blackbirds* warn young to lay low with distinctive, high, penetrating whistles as cats, stoats, magpies, jays, crows, and buzzards look for nestlings. Speckled brown young *Robins* already fend for themselves; family parties of *Long-tailed Tits* dive and call through treetops. *Blue-tits* find enough caterpillars in the oak canopy to distract them from the bird table.

A *Whitethroat* scratches and rattles away in the wet meadow below, sometimes visible on bramble tops or in halting song flight. They have been here for several weeks now along with *Blackcaps* and *Garden Warblers*. Plain, olive-green *Garden Warblers* are very different to smoke-grey, black-crowned male and rufous-capped female *Blackcaps*, but size and liquid warbling song are similar, both birds often hard to locate. One *Garden Warbler* clearly identified singing in sapling birch, moved a few feet and was thereafter impossible to locate, though in full song; less frantic, liquid cascade than *Blackcap* with more scratchy notes interspersed.

Both *Sedge Warblers* and *Reed Warblers* sing deep in wetland reeds and scrub, dry scratching interspersed with whistles. The streaked and eye-striped *Sedge Warbler* is loud and frantic, often visible in song flight or hanging on the side of reed stems; secretive, plain, soft-brown *Reed Warbler* more measured and relaxed.

A few *Mergansers* remain, offshore and in the estuary. *Shelduck* have long paired, handsome black and white with chestnut breast bands and red knobbed bills, heads sweeping low, systematically sieving molluscs from shining mud.

# *Insect Eaters* .......................................................................... 21st May

OUR LITTLE RIVER is now dancing and full of life, sparkling with sunlight. Midges yo-yo in sunbeams, visibly paired, enjoying a few minutes of aerial courtship before death, snapped up by *Wagtails*, both yellow-bellied *Grey* and black-and-white *Pied* flicking up from river boulders. Midges sail by on the bright surface, hurrying to lay their eggs before being taken with a flip by fingerling trout in fast water or marked by slow spreading rings in pools.

Everything is busy fighting for food, mates or young, recent rains followed by warm sun giving a fly bonanza for summer migrants.

At the station halt, across the tracks a *Whitethroat* spends our whole few minutes wait for the train defending territory in scratchy song: deep in sallow, white throat distended or off across the rushy meadow; back again to the ditch; up to tip-top sallow twig; then into blue sky, still rattling away in strange, halting song flight.

Blue-backed *Swallow* twitters by, patrolling the line in lilting flight, snapping flies out of the sky, tail streamers enabling low velocity flits and sweeps; a superb sight, with cream-pink breast and blood red throat.

On our return to the halt, well-fed, insectivorous summer migrants are still at it: *Willow Warbler* serenades from a high perch just up the line; *Garden Warbler* gives short stanzas from a hedgerow across the meadow; a *Sedge Warbler* scratches and rattles away, hidden in the ditch, interspersing its tirade with imitated notes of other birds.

We once spent several minutes scouring the landscape for the earliest *Yellow Wagtail* arrival ever, only to find the notes emanating from a *Sedge Warbler* in the reeds. This spring, in early April, a *Starling* played the same trick, throwing the odd *Swift* scream into its chimney pot recital, accurate enough to deceive a seasoned birder.

# *May Morning* ............................................................................. 31st May

HIGH, WHITE CLOUDS streamed overhead from the north on a cool, sunny May morning. We thought to stroll up to check the *Barn Owl* nest; perhaps finding *Redstarts* heard singing earlier. As we left, a *Blue Tit* slipped into steps wall stonework, muffled high 'peeping' denoting a hungry brood deep within. *Pied Flycatcher* gave its halting song from new territory, high in oaks above. A small movement in leaf litter, thought to be fledgling *Great Tit* turned out to be *Blackcap*, tiny form thrumming with fear and life. *Pied Flycatcher* singing in the usual garden treetops, flitted obligingly across to pirouette briefly for flies over our woodland path; striking, white and black masked aerobatics.

Out in sunny pasture, we traced *Pignut* shoots deep down in turf for knobbly, brown tubers, tasting like nutty carrot. *Willow Warblers* sang all around in woods and scrub as we walked, our voices lowered as we approached the barn.

Sure enough, in the dark, the white owl stood on narrowed legs before the nest hole; head turned to preen under pale, sandy wings, before disappearing into the cavity.

Out in the open, we moved towards repeated, hurried phrases of a *Redstart* (singing close to distant farm outbuildings. As we followed each new phrase, a *Jay* flitted up the gorse-covered bank into young oak and *Bullfinch* dived across the lane with a plaintive mew, but the *Redstart* remained elusive, eventually moving too deep into woodland to be seen. A *Goldfinch* twittered from overhanging branches to the fence top, black and gold with blood red face. Another *Redstart* sang close by, very difficult to locate in woodland.

As we left, the black and white masked form of a male *Redstart* was spotted on gorse, in the open above; robin-red tail flirted obligingly as it dived for cover.

# *Wildlife Walk* ......................................................................... 7th June

ALREADY BY 10.00AM the sun beats hot: responsible for providing a wildlife-rich experience, all is worryingly quiet. A *Swallow* preening on a wire proves a handsome subject for telescope training; red-cream flanked under lifted, blue-black wing; flashing deep red gorge. Cocky *Jackdaw* bounces into sheep pasture, bronze *Garden Chafers* buzzing all around in heat haze. Soft grey-and-cream young *Pied Wagtails* work along a wall top, not long fledged.

Above the ridge, a *Buzzard* rolls easily away from swooping *Raven*, gradually circling out of range. Further along, angular *Red Kite* soars, steering with forked tail. *Buzzard*, now flying directly towards us, suddenly folds broad wings to accelerate vertically down, disappearing legs outstretched, behind trees.

On the Maes, a *Whitethroat* scratches away in full view, a study in brown, grey and white. Two pink-breasted *Linnets* land twittering in front. A brown young *Stonechat* moves off a fence post, call like chipped flints. Last scan of the pasture finds a dun, streaked *Meadow Pipit* on a fence top and several *Skylarks* in hovering song flight, cascades of liquid notes and scratches.

On our approach, two *Shelduck* fly white and black from the salting to shining mudflats, another pair shepherding eight, downy, striped young along the further shore. A *Curlew* swims across a still tidal pool, preposterously long bill held aloft; a lone, long-legged *Redshank* bobs nervously amidst pink *Thrift*. A streak of feathers along the thrift-carpeted salting is terminated by an imperious, black-hooded *Peregrine* wings half-open over prey, like an Egyptian mural.

Skirting the tidal lagoon, two neatly-banded *Ringed Plover* move quietly amongst pebbles, scrape found later with a clutch of four. *Red-billed Oystercatcher* sits black in shingle on a single, pointed, khaki egg. Two, black-bellied, summer *Dunlin* remain perfectly camouflaged amongst tidal boulders with ten *Plover* and three very late *Whimbrel*.

# *Boat Trip* .................................................................... 14th June

THE ANNUAL Llyn Heritage Coast boat trip is exceptionally rich this year. Eleven grinning *Dolphins*, like shiny, black neoprene torpedoes, soon playing close by; barrelling, leaping and splashing all around. Backing into a black sea-cave, ledges are lined with harsh-crying, nesting seabirds: hundreds of sitting white *Kittwakes*; penguin-like, white-bellied, brown-backed *Guillemots* and black, plier-beaked *Razorbills*. Auks buzz in off the sea; *Kittiwakes* with black-tipped wings soar along the cliffs. Black *Cormorants* line cliff tops, primitive as pterodactyls; green-sheened *Shags* on lower ledges, fishing close in, or drying wings, silhouette on black rocks. *Great Black-backed Gulls* mooch about, shuffling along to drown a brown shag chick when hungry. An occasional grey *Fulmar* glides, stiff-winged along the cliff-face.

Leaving pleasure boats behind, we pass through great rafts of swimming *Manx Shearwaters* reluctantly taking off to skim the waves on stiff wings in clouds like midges over water; long-winged, long-haul, gliding versions of the busy *Guillemots*.

Backing into the bay on Ynys Enllis, *Grey Seals* bask like great blotchy bananas on rocks and shore; one furred pup laid across the stern of a rowing boat, an older, wet-suited relative circling, head aloft to find out how it was done.

Back under the great reared cliffs of the Llyn headland, black, flat-winged *Choughs* soar and sweep up the rock face into nest fissures or bounce onto the cliff top on red legs to delve or catch *Garden Chafers* with fine, red, sickle bills.

*Peregrine* rounds the headland, gliding powerfully overhead to land below the skyline; black hood and barred breast clear.

Last found, least in size: hundreds of neat *Puffins* spread over cross currents, busy swimming, diving, feeding and buzzing overhead to low cliff-top burrows amongst young *Tree Mallow*; well-known sad clown faces and rainbow parrot bills a complete privilege and joy to see.

# *Llyn y Feddw* ............................................. 21st June

SHADOWS PASS OVER a bright green landscape as a northerly breeze moves white cumulus overhead.

Tea and sandwiches packed, we are soon on the ancient drover's road, opening gates and splashing through puddled ruts, past hut circles; a gang of *Herring Gulls* snatch beetles off grassland and soar overhead on the updraft.

A dark *Buzzard* moves up the hillside; white-rumped *Wheatears* 'chack' onto stone walls; trilling *Meadow Pipits* parachute down, accelerating for a final swoop into rushes. A cloud of *Corvids* rises behind the ridge, a *Peregrine* departing unconcerned in a powerful glide around the hill.

Last gentle rise and the bright lake opens up below held in a hollow of the hill, a good ripple on the water.

Walking to the far shore, looking and listening for rising fish, *Stonechats* call from the rocky hillside; *Swallows* hawk for midges over the wave. On the shillet beach, reddish-green *Sundew* rosettes sit in bright green moss, each lobed leaf with gnat-speckled, sticky hairs.

Passing cloud turns water sky-grey; even the lee shore shows no spreading rings. On boggy rocks nearby, deep blue butterwort flowers stand like long-stemmed African violets over sticky yellow flypaper leaves.

The sun shines out and the clear mountain lake splashes as wild *Brown Trout* take wind-blown *Garden Chafers* floating by in the ripple, legs vainly waving, along with emerging gnats and midges.

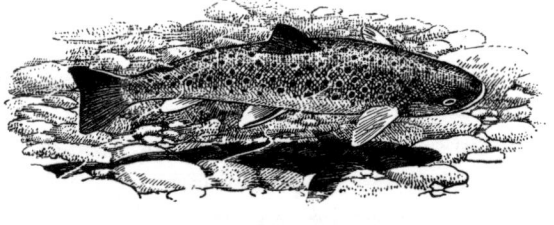

A line cast out into the ripple and pulled straight soon jerks as a trout splashes at a beetle imitation.

Many casts bring no response before a solid tug relays its electrifying message from the wild and a wild *Brown Trout* springs from the lake, predator turned prey. Quickly despatched for the smoker, trout are caught on beetle, midge and tiny gnat imitations whilst the sun shines, but feeding stops every time a cloud passes.

# *Moth Catching Notes* ............................................. 28th June

THE KIDS' GROUP arrived 9:30PM equipped with protective sunglasses for moth catching, a new activity. Expert John Hicks set up a mercury vapour lamp over a wooden box set with perspex sheets as a baffle trap, all on white sheet spread on the lawn with scattered egg boxes for shady moth refuge.

Two huge green moth nets proved popular to chase imaginary moths as light died and midges began dancing. An unsuspecting *Longhorn Sedge* was whisked from the air, pounced upon, nipped into a specimen tube and passed around for inspection in lieu of moths.

At last, a brown and buff moth: netted before it reached the trap; identified as *Barred Straw*. Next, a small, delicate, pale buff *Muslin Footman*, followed by *Carpet Moth* and *White Wave*.

Home time, the lamp left lit to work its magic overnight.

Early morning: the light was turned off and trap moved to a cool, shaded spot. Well-camouflaged moths were spread hard against the timber box, two immediately obvious: one, startlingly like a snapped twig stub; another, large, open-spread moth of pale jade.

In the afternoon, experts and kids crowded around the trap: excitement as new moths found; some frustration in transferring to specimen tubes.

Evocative names for wonderfully marked and configured insects: *Shoulder-Striped Wainscot, The Dot, Heart* and *Dart*... added to *Buff Tip* and *Emerald* (above); *Elephant Hawk Moth*, tan and pink monster; pure white, furry-bodied, black-spotted *White Ermine*, poisonous to birds; *Buff Ermine*, not poisonous but protected by imitating its white mentor; *Peppered Moth*, well-documented for melanistic black form evolved in sooty industrial areas; *Burnished Brass*, iridescent with copper, green and pink. 45 species collected, including *Grey Arches* not previously found by John. What a great privilege to be introduced to such a rich world of colour, pattern and suggestive names.

# *Duneland Summer* ............................................................. 5th July

WITH TWO SCHOOL GROUPS DUE, we check the planned route. Beside the railway, flowers are tall and rich: *Red Campion* and feathery *Horsetails* stand in bramble and nettle; purple *Buddleia* sprawls over stone walls; pale-yellow *Mullein* towers grey-felted from cracked tarmac. Crossing the tracks, the path meanders through dense, seeding grasses: *Whitethroat* rattles in *Sallow* scrub; *Meadow Pipit* parachutes its song flight.

Entering the dunes, grasses thin giving space for late, single, pale-yellow *Burnet Roses* set in delicate, ferny foliage; a bank carpeted with pink Thyme cerise; stars of grass-high *Maiden Pink*: *Sand Leek* heads stand like metallic pink drum sticks.

At the top of the beach, two *Ringed Plover* work frantically to distract the dog from two downy young running long-legged along the dune base for cover. Sand streams along the beach and tiers of creamy surf swarm off shore in stormy sunshine.

Climbing back through soft sand with stiff *Marram* tufts, glaucous *Sea Holly* buds just opening powder blue; lax, lemon yellow *Evening Primrose* splits reddish buds; white and pink striped *Sea Bindweed* sprawls between *Marram* stems. Leaving tumultuous wind and waves behind, we descend into a peaceful, open bowl set in the dunes: level floored, a carpet of fine grasses and wild flowers with *Sallow* scrub in damp spots. *Pyramidal Orchids* stand like deep cerise candles; yellow *Vetch* and *Dune Pansy* backdrop to deep powder blue *Sheep's Bit* heads; pale meringue tongues of *Marsh Helleborine* stand in lax spires in *Creeping Willow* and *Dewberry*) starry *Eyebright* set in crinkled leaved towers in the turf with tiny white *Fairy Flax* floating over; *Self Heal* heads stand red, flowers like blue-lipped embers protruding. No *Bee Orchids* just yet, but even white and *Red Clover* heads look exceptional when one's eyes are attuned to this world of bright colour, form and structure.

# Summer Foraging ................................................................ 12th July

THE YEAR IS TURNING as leaves harden up, losing their spring lustre; fledgling birds blunder from hedgerows, adults dishevelled from raising broods or moulting. *Curlews* are returning to the estuary with a few *Redshank*; two *Dunlin* have remained in black-bellied breeding plumage through summer instead of nesting in moors.

*Glasswort* or *Marsh Samphire* is good eating right now; salty, succulent leaves standing in salt-washed grass and tidal flats. It can be eaten fresh, boiled fast and served with melted butter like asparagus, or pickled in good, spiced vinegar, stem pulled through teeth to remove succulent leaves. Pickled *Samphire* is traditionally sold by fishmongers, these days supplied from Israel. To harvest, cut the stem with secateurs above the lowest leaves to ensure plant survival. The name *Glasswort* derives from sixteenth century use for glass making, ash providing impure carbonate of soda to mix with sand.

*Golden Samphire* is a yellow maritime daisy, also with thick, fleshy leaves to survive salt conditions, but not edible. *Rock Samphire* is a yellow flowered Umbellifer a plant family that includes cow parsley, hogweeds, and many vegetables including carrot, parsnip and celery. Growing on cliffs rather than marshes, this was traditionally gathered along with gull's eggs. The trade only faded in Victorian times due to adulteration with other plants, cheaper and safer to harvest. The plant fresh picked is lemon fragrant and may be steamed and served with butter or pickled as with *Marsh Samphire*, the fleshy parts sucked away from stringy veins.

First Agaricus macrosporus *Mushrooms* have been gathered from sheep pasture. Examined carefully and tasted raw, all seemed well, a judgement confirmed by the delicious smell and taste when fried in oil and by this subsequent diary entry. Looking forward to *Field & Horse Mushrooms* found at the same location in a few weeks.

# *Bright & Fresh* ......................................................................... 19th July

DESPITE MEDIA REPORTS, we have enjoyed some wonderful days: cumulus, white in bright sun and blue skies; dark blue nimbus over mountains; light hard and clear after rain.

On the estuary, *Terns* bleating prompts scan over blue lagoon, sand bars wet from receding tide. Black-capped *Sandwich Terns* beat upwind in lilting flight, hawking for sand eels, white wings bright in sun against dark cloud. Far away, at the estuary outfall, a tiny tern moves fast, to and fro, jetting into the water; first *Little Tern* of the year, fraction the size of nearby *Sandwich Terns*.

Weather fine to fish in the afternoon: new lake with boat; lilies and water lobelia encroaching from shallow margins. No rises in dark waves, just a few splashes in the weed. 'Daddy-long-legs' imitations fail to raise a fish: perhaps still too early.

Young *Peregrine* wanders the sky calling for food, later joined by an adult with flickering flight below bright cumulus and dark nimbus. Trying damsel nymph and water beetle imitations under water, line tugs and bends the rod, twanging as the fish dives under the boat; a beautifully marked *Brown Trout*, taken on 'Haul y Gwynt', a traditional Welsh black pattern.

On return, the landowner had kindly left a bag of mushrooms on the running board. Driving through bright green, sunlit woods, pale orange *Chanterelle* is spotted in moss. A search brings a bagful: fresh, apricot trumpets, enough to fill 6 terrines, fried and covered in butter with garlic and lemon zest.

An unexpected opportunity to fish that evening brings first *Sewin* of the year, tight under the far bank at last light; narrow, silver form taut with power. A *Bat* hit the rod tip, dropping into the water: wading rescue unnecessary as it motored to the bank without hesitation, shoulders oaring sunken wings.

# *Summer Rain* ........................................................................ 26th July

TWO INCHES OF RAIN, 24 gallons per square yard, recorded between a fine Thursday and the sun's return on Saturday; not exceptional here with an annual rainfall of 40", the river frequently higher. *Sea Trout* are still moving and a good bag of mushrooms collected Sunday morning gave a superb Monday lunch of *Sewin* and field mushrooms fried in butter with brown bread.

Fishing on a mountain lake saw a bright, gusty start, loud with wind rush and sluicing outfall. Green aquatic damsel nymphs brave hunting trout to swim to emergent stems and rocks for transformation to electric blue adults. Nymph imitations surprised a few trout as the day passed through streaming rain to steaming sun. The wind changed a full 180' then died completely, perfect rocky crag reflections broken only by spreading rings of rising trout as we left.

At Llandanwg, an exceptional flock of *Gannets* first seen from inland: adults wings black-tipped, pure white against blue sky; juveniles grey-brown. The flock of many hundreds settled on a tidal race off *Mochras*, a few birds moving back up tide. Rock-pooling that afternoon, a similar great flock of dark *Manx Shearwaters* swung low over the sea, loosely spread across the entire horizon. A single *Whimbrel* stood clear and proud on the beach, presumably a returning bird only weeks after the last spring migrants left in June; much lighter flight than the *Curlew* on the salting, buff crown stripes clear in the hard light.

At home, enjoying peaceful last light, occasional flitting brought attention to a black winged bat hawking in the room, soft fluttering only with confined turns. Flipping up to hang from a joist, it twirled left and right, licking clean black wings, chest and shoulders: small, black winged and pale bellied with medium length ears, possibly *Lesser Horseshoe*.

# *Turn of the Year* .................................................. 2nd August

SECOND MUSHROOM PICKING; blackberries ripe; early morning nip with *Robins* singing and 'ticking', territorial behaviour resuming as red breasts return: turn of the season confirmed. *Curlews* and *Redshank* gather in the estuary; *Whimbrels* on the shore feed and rest on their journey from northern nesting grounds to sub-Saharan winter quarters; individual *Whitethroats*, *Sedge Warblers* and *Redstart* spotted on the Maes, also heading south.

*Starlings*, *Goldfinches*, *Greenfinches* and *Wagtails* are forming sizeable flocks for winter. *Starling* party squawks off in tight formation; *Curlew* flock rises in alarm, resettling on the salting; bleating *Sandwich Tern* flock lifts off the sand bar, elegant darts of pure white, alighting closer to receding tide: all separate signs of a passing winged threat. A slate grey form speeds across the Maes, encumbered by talon-held prey, alighting facing away on an estuary boulder not 50 yards distant, wings part-mantled over a dark form, despite the proximity of our party. An irate *Herring Gull* speeds over the strand causing the *Peregrine* to depart, still gaping *Starling* gripped tight behind.

On the shore, after at least two attempts, a pair of *Ringed Plover* has raised a single chick. Despite bold black and white banding, the adults are superbly camouflaged, a short, quiet, plaintive whistle first sign of their presence. Locating parents amongst boulders or weed-strewn strand, best to stand back and wait. Soon, amongst pale grey, rounded boulders, a tiny, similarly pale grey form materialises as chick moves closer to parent or to a warmer or more secure spot. Not long after, as adults preen or doze, often standing on one orange leg, the chick will peck for sand hoppers or stretch fluffy wing stubs in the sun. Each quick movement is followed by static intervals when fluffy chick turns to stone as *Herring Gulls* patrol the dune face.

# *Lilliput* .......................................................................... 9th August

DESPITE 'DOOM AND GLOOM' about the weather and early signs of autumn, we have had wonderful weather this week.

Wednesday seas were flat, oily-calm with delicate white *Sandwich Terns* wheeling and darting into the sea right at the water's edge; occasional sea trout leapt, silver-gold bar thrashing high into the air before splash-down. Way across the bay, bright white, black-winged *Gannets* patrol the blue water for fish; a lone Porpoise quietly barrels for air in a strip of dark, breeze-ruffled water.

This week, two elegant *Godwits* join *Whimbrel* and *Redshank* in the brown, weed-strewn, golden boulders of the shore where numbers of *Dunlin* and *Ringed Plover* are building. The young *Ringed Plover* raised at the head of the beach has grown from woolly, imitation grey stone to downy version of its parents in just a week, standing stock-still on boulders or bobbing in alarm just like the adults.

In the dunes, *Marsh Helleborines* still stand in good numbers, typical orchid flowers, thick petalled cream and buff like icing sugar. Earlier orchids seem burnt, setting seed on brown stems and dying leaves. Delicate white *Fairy Flax*, drifts of starry *Eyebright*; deep yellow, occasionally orange *Trefoils* still in full flower in rabbit-grazed turf; pink and white *Rest-Harrow* spreads into bare sand with dusty, furry leaves. Last, deep *Yellow-Rattle* flowers among dry bladder seed capsules; Sheep's Bit tatters and fades in blue; shiny, thick, green fruit has replaced delicate lemon *Evening Primrose* blooms; polished brown-black *Burnet Rose* hips shine from ferny foliage.

A wonderful pale orange *Kaffir Lily*, flown some garden as a seed, thrives high on a bare dune in hot sun. Dark pink *Thyme* covers warm banks with aromatic carpets, foamy yellow *Ladies' Bedstraw* interspersed; common *Daisy* and *Red Clover* heads look suddenly huge in this Lilliputian world of tiny perfection.

# *Rockpooling* ......................................................... 16th August

STANDING NEXT TO THE SIGNBOARD, a family group in waterproofs and bare knees stand in the grey drizzle, Dad wincing as the vehicle swings into view.

The assumption that everyone is ready for action causes an instant negative reaction from one small boy and hasty indications from the Mums that two middle-sized lads are the motivating force, a rueful Dad detailed to accompany. So, kitted up with aquarium tanks and nets, we set off to a grey, misty and deserted beach, eagerly discussing what might be found and what hazards we need to be aware of.

*Sandwich Terns* hawk and dart into the water just off shore, only a shade less grey than the sea.

An abundance of large, transparent brown *Prawns* is immediately obvious, blue and yellow striped legs visible in the aquaria. *Sand Gobies* jet from cover, relying on almost perfect camouflage for defence, persuaded once spotted to shoot into a net. Dad, carrying the aquaria, jumps visibly when approached from behind by his lad with a black and orange shore crab as big as the tank. Conical Limpets and snail-like molluscs add to the collection: shiny black Winkles in clusters; flat, grey-striped, Turk's cap Top Shells; deep yellow Flat Periwinkles inching over brown *Bladder Wrack*; an occasional blue mussel rooted to a rock.

Excitement runs high as dark *Blennies* flip and splash in one pool, shooting to hide under rocks or weed, lower fins adapted for wriggling overland, eyes high and frog-like.

Starfish are elusive even on the lower shore, only one small coral pink form found under a boulder, but jelly red, blue fringed Beadlet Anemones hang abundant on undersides of rocks, venomous tentacles surprisingly deadly even to small fish. *Terns*' shallow water fishing is explained as fine, green and silver *Sand Eels* dart in lower pools.

# *Chanterelles* ............................................................. 23rd August

RECENT RAINS bring a third picking of fine orange chanterelles in deep green moss over rock in light shade. Chalky hedgehog mushrooms are another, edible species found conveniently alongside, pointed out by another keen local forager. *Wild Damsons* spatter the lane. One local *Crab Apple* is laden with ripening fruit, another small tree with branches so densely packed, few leaves can be seen.

Young *Buzzards* have been calling loudly for food for weeks, perched in trees or circling valleys and woods.

On the shore, fawn brown young *Herring Gulls* make a whistling version of the same call and young *Sandwich Tern* squeaks are distinguishable from bleating adults. At last count, 185 *Sandwich Terns* rested, slept or preened on boulders at the water-line, amongst them several *Black Headed Gulls* with red legs, black heads reduced for winter to marks behind the eye. On one boulder, a small gull preened with pale yellow bill, short black legs and ink-dipped wing tips: *Kittiwakes* nest on cliff ledges across the bay but are rarely seen on this sandy shore, this the first sighting of the year.

*Gulls* and *Terns* seem white in the sun until an adult *Gannet* soars by, seven-foot span of black tipped, brightest white, quartering a wind-whipped, dark blue sea.

*Rabbit* cropped, fine turf of the Maes holds a scattering of *Pied Wagtails, Meadow Pipits* and *Wheatears*, with *Stonechats* on the turf or cocked atop some high point. *Linnets* and *Goldfinches* twitter in the gorse and *Greenfinches* in dune planted Rosa rugosa.

Every *Pied Wagtail*, from grey and buff young to striking black and white adult, is a potential *White Wagtail*, but when a *White Wagtail* appears there is no mistake. Grey back and wings give prominence to white markings, breast and flanks, a subtle difference that makes clear the name.

# *Whimbrel* ........................................................... 30th August

SPECIES NUMBERS BUILD as winter visitors returning to estuary and bay overlap with summer migrants stopping by on the way south.

Olive green and pale woodland warblers flit in dune planted rose sprays, briefly visible as they snap up insects along the fence line. Elegant *Wheatears* stand buff-peach and tall on cropped turf and boulder tops, flashing squared white rump and tail in sweeping flight, down from mountain stone wall nest sites before moving south.

*Common Sandpipers* also appear in the estuary in spring and autumn between migration and nesting by mountain lakes, distinctive piping heard from afar, confirmed by distinctive bobbing and characteristic down-winged flight low over water. Other waders and ducks bob heads when nervous, particularly *Redshank*; *Common Sandpipers* bob and rock the whole time.

A pair of *Bar-Tailed Godwits* accompanies the gathering *Curlew* flock: one bird russet with residual summer plumage; the other in grey-silver winter garb; both with long, pink-based, slightly upturned bills. *Curlew*, *Redshank* and *Godwits* over-winter on the estuaries, as do increasing numbers of neat *Ringed Plover* and busy *Dunlin*, several *Dunlin* still in black-bellied, russet breeding plumage, the rest silver-grey with black bills and legs.

Following four *Teal* breasting the waves off-shore last week, there are now more *Mallard* in the estuary than in winter, still in eclipse plumage, amongst them a smaller bird, fading russet, long wings crossed at the tip, first of hundreds of *Wigeon* that will return by winter. On the shore, *Whimbrel* are elusive amongst bronze and green weed-coated boulders, merely passing through on their way from northern tundra to sub-Saharan winter quarters, spotted only when they move or briefly silhouette against bright sea or sand.

Beyond, a straggling line of black duck denotes returning *Common Scoter*, thousands of which over-winter in the bay, thus designated a marine reserve.

# *September Fly-fishing* ............... 5th September

**BLUE SKY, HIGH CIRRUS,** and westerly breeze: a good afternoon to fish the mountain lakes.

Unease at time out of a working week passes at the first gate of the old, green, drover's road. The panorama from Bardsey to Snowdon clears the mind and lifts the heart. Daddy-long-legs drift across the breeze, legs a-dangle, kicked up from grass and rushes; tempting for trout as they skid onto water; encouraging for fly-fishermen after a lean August.

The lake opens out below, blue reflected sky ruffled by breeze. No rise seen or heard whilst tying on a large Daddy-long-legs and a variety of small midge imitations as found in the last catch. Walk the lee shore looking for rises, kicking 'Daddies' out across the water from rushes. Casting into the ripple: as ever, hope and optimism firming to gritty realism within the hour; more artificial midges tried in every combination, through quiet patches and sporadic rises.

Eventually, splashy rises indicate fish feeding on 'Daddies' blown off the hillside. A trout leaps for an artificial. Again, and the hook bites. Nice to catch, but nothing learned. A trial of 3 'Daddy' patterns brings no results, confirmation of summer inconsistency.

Later, the breeze drops to give a patch of rises in casting range, none of which trout prove interested in the finest Daddy-long-legs. After yet another 'last cast', resolve grows to reel in. Top flies removed, only a 3mm, white-winged 'Angler's Curse' imitation remains on the point. With even smaller white midges whizzing over the water below, it is worth another 'last cast' at a recent rise. One pull to straighten the line and 'bang', a trout breaks the surface.

Satisfaction in finding another fly for summer is tempered by lack of time to test consistency; motivation to come up again, were any needed.

# *The Great Ash* .................................................. 14th September

THIS WEEK WAS SPENT around the Wye and Usk rivers looking at gardens and estates.

Parkland oaks and cedars planted in the eighteenth and nineteenth centuries are now magnificent specimens. Victorians planted their gardens with exotic species discovered and imported from empire as well as new varieties selected for unusual colour, texture or form.

The established method of estimating tree age is by measuring the girth at chest height, equating inches to years and amending this initial estimate by addition or subtraction according to the vigour of species and observed tree maturity, situation and health. Two healthy *Atlantic Cedars* and a *Copper Beech* planted c.1900 in the same location each measured girths of 145 inches. This is surprising on two counts: firstly, that the *Copper Beech*, a broadleaved hardwood, grew in this case at the same rate as coniferous, softwood Cedars; secondly, that the girths of all three are more than 25% greater than the expected average.

Regardless of numbers and theories, these great trunks supporting the weight of enormous crowns inspire with their scale, stability, resilience and strength.

Trees here in Ardudwy, growing in shallow, rocky soils, often wind pruned on exposed slopes or coastal strip, seldom attain great dimensions, but there is a great, round crowned, stump-boled *Ash* set in a long hollow, sheltered between two woodland belts, with a girth of 250 inches; greater than any listed. A few limbs have crashed out at some point, and bracket fungus shows heart rot, so this tree now lacks the vigour of those described above. According to the theory, this tree was planted around 1750, a time that saw the start of Methodism, education and industrial revolution in Wales. The tree's true age will only be discovered if and when the tree is felled and the annual rings counted.

# *Early Autumn* .................................................. 20th September

WITH GROUND FROST REPORTED on low ground, the season takes a sudden turn to autumn, leaves turning colour and gathering windblown in gutters and sheltered spots. Deciduous trees close off nutrient flow from branch to leaf, halting green chlorophyll production, leaving red anthocyanins and yellow carotenes to light up woods and landscape in a final flare of colour before dead of winter.

*Swallows* and *Sand Martins* still sweep low over the Maes and dunes for insects or hawk and flit high over the ridge beyond, tiny slips of black in great skies of wind, sunlight, and ominous cloud over dark mountains. Sailor blue and white *House Martins* are gone from the village, following screaming *Swifts* that left weeks ago. *Warblers* are still moving south with occasional *Chiffchaff* couplets on the wind and a tan and grey *Whitethroat* working a bramble for insects.

Numbers of waders and wildfowl are building in the estuary. Small numbers of *Teal* and *Wigeon* have returned, still in nondescript 'eclipse' plumage, males awaiting bold designs of American Indian colours, so striking in winter. Drake *Mallard* springing from Rush clumps are ahead of the game, white collar clearly separating dark, iridescent head and neck from soft grey back and silver flanks. *Redshank* run and feed busily on lipstick orange legs over shining mud; *Curlew* doze or preen on the salting turf or with only heads visible in the creeks. A pair of elegant *Godwit* feed and fly with *Curlews*; a single, dumpy *Knot* works shallow margins with smaller *Dunlin*, some silver grey, others with remnant summer russet and black belly. Many further grey *Knot* huddle, almost indistinguishable from shoreline boulders, with a scattering of bold *Ringed Plover*, scaly backed *Dunlin*, *Turnstones* mottled for winter. Only *Oystercatchers* are clearly visible, fussing and peeping in black, white and red.

# *Peregrine* ........................................ 26th September

OUT ON THE MAES on a bright, showery day, a *Grey Wagtail* slips, lemon bellied, around the corner of a muddy drain. Reaching the spot, no *Wagtail* is visible down the shining zigzag channel, nor on green salting.

Looking again, beyond the drain, on the bend of the ebbing estuary, a slate-grey, sharp-winged form sweeps low over grey water, fluttering at each turn to swoop again over a particular spot, like a falconer's bird at the lure. The telescope finds a wader in the water, struggling to keep head and long bill aloft, wings unused to swimming, ducking as black-hooded, sharp-winged death swoops low.

We move too fast to look long at *Wheatears* flitting ahead, flirting white tails along the dyke, or a young *Buzzard* leaving a gatepost.

Closer now, pinkish base to long bill, medium size and visible plumage identifies the struggling victim as a *Bar-Tailed Godwit*, one of two lately associated with the *Curlew* flock. Five *Mallard* swim close to mob an instinctively recognised predator.

We approach too close and the *Peregrine* flickers across to the far salting, pale streaked breast contrasting with slate-grey wings, black hood with white cheeks. As we retreat, the *Godwit* reaches shining mud shore, wings fluttered high to dry: no visible injury but too sodden for flight. The *Peregrine* leans forward, keen and alert for an opportunity to complete a botched execution.

Turning again, we miss the kill.

Now standing, still alert for danger, with yellow talons gripped on the prostrate bird, the *Peregrine* rips the breast with a strong, hooked bill, notched like secateurs, and bolts back fresh red meat. By the time we leave, the mud is bare of predator and prey, the going missed like the kill, presumably moved to a safer spot as soon as light enough to carry.

# *Merlin* ......................................................................... 4th October

AGAINST A GREY SKY, a dark form wings straight and true across a pale, still, tide-filled lagoon. Too small for *Peregrine*; too sharp-winged for *Sparrowhawk*, the raptor—now set on a far shore post—is obviously dark brown, not *Kestrel* tan: probably female *Merlin*; possibly juvenile *Sparrowhawk*: a fine sight, whatever the species.

Later, in the afternoon, we approach the estuary across rushes, creeks and salt-washed turf. The estuary bank is protected by imported rocks, a group of three standing silhouette against shining mud beyond. Almost too late, a narrow, vertical projection of the largest rock is noticed only 40 yards distant. Binoculars confirm our smallest falcon, a brown barred, female *Merlin*, bright and fearless, close enough to fill the telescope view. We move forward carefully another 10 yards, stopping when the bird shifts into profile. Bright, black lenses hold us in view between glances at the wider landscape, alert for danger and small birds. *Meadow Pipits* are the *Merlin* staple, both in moorland nest sites and estuary winter haunts, though prey ranges from insects and tiny *Goldcrests* through to *Lapwing* when opportunity arises. Our bird bobs its head nervously and soon flips out of sight over the bank, emerging to cross the estuary and settle upright out on the salting opposite.

Later, returning down the breakwater to the shore, a dark form whisks over the bank ahead and clatters into a group of boulders. The upper-parts of a brown *Merlin* remain visible amongst grey boulders as a couple stroll close by on the beach, oblivious. We approach carefully, enjoying closer looks, hoping to find the subject of the attack, but our little lady suddenly flicks up to dune height, suddenly twisting to snatch upwards with talons at something unseen against the sky before dropping behind the dunes.

# *Departures & Arrivals* ......................... 11th October

FOR MANY WEEKS, the Maes has been busy with *Finches, Wagtails*, and *Pipits* gathering into winter flocks, and *Swallows, Martins*, and *Wheatears* feeding up for migration.

*Merlin* and *Sparrowhawk* have largely cleared open areas: only *Starlings* left gathering on the wires, remaining *Pipits* and *Wagtails* keeping flight to a minimum. *Swallows* all left together, only stragglers now passing through; *Wheatear* passage is coming to an end.

The *Peregrine* on the estuary has not had the same impact on returning flocks of waders and wildfowl, numbers of *Wigeon* now in the hundreds. The whistling calls of *Wigeon* are wonderfully evocative of winter, sounds like stones skimmed on ice. Returning *Wigeon* and *Teal* are not yet restored to the bold, American Indian colours and designs of winter plumage.

Out in the bay, saw-billed, chestnut-quiffed *Mergansers* are also returning, as are *Red-Throated Divers*, silver and grey with up-tilted bills, some still in dark summer plumage. *Great Crested Grebes* are distinguished by shorter bodies and snake necks, some with remnant chestnut crests. A few, dumpy, *Little Grebes* always over-winter in the estuary; a group of five seen in the week is unusual.

Last week, exceptionally still sea conditions saw much activity on the bay. Urgent, raucous calls of many excited *Herring Gulls* were heard across the Maes. From the breakwater, the flock made a great white streak across the bay with a definite core of activity. Through the telescope, gulls lifted up and dropped repeatedly into one 'hot spot': diminutive, pied, *Razorbills* and silver *Herring Gulls* spread wide left and right. Close to shore, *Black-Headed Gulls* were also dropping excitedly into patches of water seething and boiling with fish. With no signs of *Dolphins, Porpoise* or *Seals*, this must be caused by predator fish snapping up from below through swirling balls of panicked prey.

# *Dolphins* .................................................................... 18th October

THE SEASON MOVES ON as warm, wet, southerly airflow turns to clear, cold nights. A late party of *Swallows* hawk for flies over gorse, feeding as they move south, twittering song a distillation of summer. The lilting flight of these elegant, cream-breasted, blood-throated, thin streaks of blue-black will be missed as they swoop, skim low or lift in flittering stalls and turns.

A single, high, thin whistle denotes a loose party of *Redwings* moving south on the same track, high over trees and berried thorns, calling to maintain the flock as they pass over in measured, lark-like flight. As autumn bites, parties of *Siskins* with wheezy calls and *Redpolls* with harsher notes twitter overhead in bouncing flight, looking for seed of *Larch* and *Alder* cones.

Thrushes, larks and finches are with us for winter, moving from high altitudes and latitudes and from a cold continent to this warm, maritime island. Similarly, waders and wildfowl on the estuary are attracted by ice-free winter-feeding, as are divers, grebes and sea duck out in the bay.

The October sea is still warm from summer. Just offshore, *Bass* still turn silver flanks and splash in patches of water seething with panicked baitfish. Mullet streak still water with dorsal triangles and small *Sea Trout* spring high, flipping silver in the air before splashdown.

A *Grey Seal* works its way along shore, head showing intermittently not 10 yards out. About a mile offshore, a black-finned back curves out of a grey sea, followed by another as two *Dolphins* move steadily northwards. A family ahead on the beach—backs to the sea—have not seen them. Surprised to be alerted by a panting, heavy-booted, gesticulating ornithologist running towards them on a deserted beach; seriously nervous after five minutes hard scanning shows only an empty sea.

# *Late Season Bass* ............................................................ 24th October

AIR MOVEMENT REMAINS from the south with barometric pressure high, but nights are colder with morning frost. Weather ranges daily from bright sun to cloud, sea no longer flat calm. After several weeks' intense activity, *Sea Bass* have moved on, no longer splashing the surface as they turn and slice through boiling shoals of baitfish.

Managed to fish before they left, tackling up in morning sun with an autumnal bite in the air, travelling light up the beach to trace and follow the shoals. Negotiating the boulders toward the estuary mouth, fins and tails of *Grey Mullet* cut the smooth water close to shore. Cast a maggot imitation as sand-fly larvae, hoping to tempt fish that feed mainly on microscopic life. Occasional large grey fish were visible swimming along inside waves as they towered, small fry flashing silver ahead.

Waist deep in the sea, still casting for *Mullet*, a patch turned dark as baitfish skittered green and silver across the surface, *Bass* tails swirling behind, almost too close to cast: definitely time to change the fly. A Sandeel-sized, blue-and-silver streamer brought no tug when dropped into the fishes' path; tried a white lure with coloured glitter strands worked in. At the third cast to a *Bass* turning just along the shore, the line locked solid. Powerful runs for open sea brought fears for knots, line whipping out between finger and rod held high to avoid boulders. Five minutes intense excitement working the fish to shore eventually netted a satisfying, heavy, grey and silver *Bass*.

Tide and sea conditions moved on, *Bass* activity slowed, sun too thin to warm after a good soaking, so homeward bound, very happy. Steamed in foil for 30 minutes, stuffed with dill and lemon, fresh *Bass* fed four the next evening, with sauce of Wild Sorrel.

# *Autumn Woodland* .................................................. 1st November

WOODS ON OUR VALLEY SIDES are at their autumn best, enriching overcast days, ablaze in sunshine: tight-packed, dense mounds of burnt sugar brown *Oaks* with *Ash* and *Birch* yellows; pasture bright green in contrast. Rich smells of fungus, mould and rot mingle with musk of fly-blown Ivy on woodland paths; bright crimson Rose hips spray over *Bramble*; necklaces of wax red *Bryony* hang in rain-dropped loops and swags. Bare *Apple* trees hold crabs like baubles all over, silhouette against the sky or delicate yellow amongst leaves beneath. Black pocks will simmer with the rest, to strain pale green juice that never fails to turn marmalade orange at the last minute.

Sloes here are poor this year, most bushes with only mummified fruit. Blue-bloomed sloes on one bush are all the more satisfying to pick as a consequence, dense enough to pull off in clusters; just up the lane, another with especially round, shiny black berries. Freezing breaks the skins and forms sugars to bottle with gin or vodka and sugar with time to decant for a sweet, pink, Christmas drink.

Steep valley sides and the scarp slope marking the Llanbedr Series of slate and mudstone both grow a dense cover of predominantly *Oak* and *Hazel*, generally small stature previously attributed to poor soils and salt sea winds. Interesting that turn of the century postcards show a clear skyline and slopes of well kempt pasture.

Drystone-walls within the woods seem to confirm that we may be looking at the early stages of woodland colonisation of redundant pasture, hence the even size and growth. Bracken turns to *Bramble* that protects seedling trees from grazing; first, light *Birch*, *Willow* and *Alder*; later, *Oak* and *Ash*, the occasional tree or stand of greater stature remnant of times past when grazing land was of value.

# High Rhinogs ................................................................ 8th November

THE ANNUAL 'RHINOG HORSESHOE' fell-race over: time once again to collect orienteering checkpoints from the mountaintops. Absolutely still, clear morning: sky, orange over the ridge; bracken, autumn brown; grass and rushes dew wet.

Meet the sun rising on the ridge; small wild ponies graze just below the highest peak. A flesh coloured balloon sways incongruously over a mossy bog, satin ribbon leading to a burst companion in the rushes. Cutting the ribbon, the freed partner drifts away, lifting steadily to clear the next ridge, peach against a greying sky.

Superb views over the sea and Llyn Peninsula: scarcely a breeze, even on the top. Steep descent on the next ridge: a tarn below mirrors the sky; a few ripples but no rings from rising trout. Only the rattle of stones dislodged on the descent and distinctive 'clock-clock' call as a *Raven* flip rolls overhead.

On the climb, the dog herds *Wild Goats* that stand at bay, close on a rocky outcrop. The last peak cleared, a track of peat and stone leads away through heather and rock and a *Woodcock* starts up, russet-brown on broad wings, close enough to note heavy bill and peaked brow.

Down in the Bwlch—'Door of Ardudwy' in English—a *Wren's* harsh call and loud song echoes, urgent in the rocky ravine. The track follows a stream out to the valley.

Three hunters in camouflage are out to cull wild goats, with rifles, telescopic sights and tripods for a clean kill. Both ravine and goats are mentioned by Thomas Pennant in his 'Tour in Wales' written in 1780; 'Coch yr Wden' the Welsh for hung goat eaten with cheese compounded of milk of cow and sheep. The goats are shaggy and bi-coloured; males with magnificent heavy horns, straight up and flared back high.

# *Tracks* ......................................................................... 15th November

ON THE DESK IS A SMALL PLAQUE of off-white, chalky composition with smooth sides, top surface irregular and sandy with clear raised print in the centre, like a WD arrow with the apex lost.

Not only does this disc bring memories of a sunny, autumn afternoon and sandy estuary where it was cast, but the splay and bow of sharp toes speak clearly of the *Redshank* that made the mark, running about on lipstick crimson legs, busily scanning the shore, prodding sands with sharp, red-tipped bill for crustaceans, molluscs and worms before sweeping off fast and low with loud piping calls, blazing sudden white wing bars, rump and tail.

Another plaque holds a larger, deeper print, each scale visible, slight web between two toes, the memory of a muddy creek in the estuary salting, and a picture of the more stately, splayed gait of knobbly-kneed *Curlew*, deep holes made by improbably long curved bills in the mud, and of loud bubbling notes that echo across the marsh or sound down winter winds.

A similar sized print with impossibly thin toes, bowed inwards by a web faintly marked between, brings to mind a small party of *Wigeon* emerging from tidal estuary to graze, heads down over algae-strewn *Samphire*; superbly marked, coloured males, heads occasionally lifted to check sky and marsh for danger, rushing to water with yelps and whistles on white panelled wings if alarmed.

A simple pack with proprietary powdered filler, plastic drinks bottle, scissors and spoon are all that is required, the bottle cut into rings to frame each print and form the mould, base used to mix the filler, top and neck to scoop water for the mix. Prints in sand cure in about 60 minutes, much more quickly than those in mud; both faster in warmer temperatures.

# *Winter Light* ............................................................. 22nd November

EARLY START ON THE MAES: grey sky paling with mountains dark in inky cloud. *Little Egret* breasts a keen east breeze along the dune tops, cream in early light, black legs trailing, hind toe projected up behind.

On the estuary the light is still low, wind too cold to stand for long. *Wigeon*, *Teal*, and *Curlew* roost, silhouette against shining mud, only *Redshank* running lightly or stopping to probe with thin bills; even bold marked *Shelduck* and white *Mute Swans* are dull in dreary morning light. A female *Merganser*, ginger quiff ruffled, is blown downwind in leaden chop; *Ringed Plover* stand like ticks on wind-dried sand.

Suddenly, estuary and roosting *Wigeon* are washed yellow as winter sun gleams from dark mountain cloud. Soon, exquisite, silver edged, black feathers laid over silver flanks are enjoyed in true colour as a male *Wigeon* fills the telescope view, walking sedately with his duck, buff striped russet head held high.

Off the exposed breakwater, *Turnstones* creep on short orange legs amongst boulders where *Oystercatchers* roost, bold black, white and red; occasional black *Scoter* lifts into sight in gunmetal-grey waves beyond; a *Shag* stands in classical pose on a great rock along the shore.

Suddenly, waders stream off with agitated calls over the sea and a pack of *Wigeon* close to shore lifts briefly to settle in waves further off. Tiny *Dunlin* streak along the strand, pale against the sea, turning white bellied as a flock in morning light.

No *Peregrine* sighted, despite the signs.

Where dunes shelter the beach and water beyond, two female *Goosander* snorkel and submerge in shallows only two waves from shore, brown-ginger head feathers cut sharp in distinctive 'bob' behind, occasionally kicking up white spray in chasing display with lowered heads.

The *Shag* remains in erect pose as we pass.

# *Grayling* .................................................................................... 27th November

INLAND TO FISH THE DEE for winter *Grayling*: sunlit green pasture contrasting with russet, reds and gold, winter-bright, dusty skin of Bala Lake, creased with slow currents.

Walking the riverbank, a lone *Wigeon* springs from the slack, pale belly flared in a climbing turn before whistling away on needle sharp wings and tail. A long, streamy run is combed for *Grayling*, flicking the line upstream and leading it down to sink and bounce the flies along the bottom, waiting for the current to bear them up at the end. Not a twitch, even from small fry that often take the topmost fly. Exploring deeper water and a tight runnel round the bend, a *Dipper*, sat on a rock under a high bank, murmurs and scratches to itself, quiet but perfectly audible over the rush of water; still no sudden tug on the line.

Below a wide, stone arched bridge, winter sunlit water kicks and splashes across the weir, welling up and creasing as it spreads into the bright pool below. Just off the bank where oncoming waters pass left and right, beneath the folds and wrinkles of up-welling waters, occasional, subsidiary lines seem to form. Cast out into oncoming waters: line hard to see in bright, winter sun and retrieve not easy to match the current, but the twitch on the line under the rod tip is unmistakeable. Lifting for the third cast, the line locks solid, then quivers and comes free as a long, pale fish breaks the surface. Though a Salmonid, Grayling is armoured with scales and sports a great sail of a ruby-tinged dorsal fin when erect. The scales gleam palest gold, like winter sun, with a faint wisp of iridescence. Above pouting, under-slung mouth, the eye, ringed pale bronze, holds a strange, irregular, black ink-drop pupil.

# *December Gales* .......................................... 5th December

GALES AND DRIVING RAIN of past weeks give little to report until recently. One black night, sash window lowered for air, rain spattered on glass, rush of river in flood and wind in trees. Then, overhead in the dark: soft fluttering, occasional scratches and scrabbles and a whack of something hitting the lantern light shade. Light lit, a small black *Bat* hit the wall and fell, wings outstretched, behind ornaments on the mantelpiece. Light off again, soft fluttering resumed, we share our shelter.

At the beach car park, the vehicle rocks, rain spattered, in the gale. *Curlew* beat overhead against the storm; *Kestrel* flips from a gatepost, sweeps low over the Maes and away. Below dark, heavy cloud, white wisps drift across mountain-tops with glimpses of snow. Wrapped up tight against the weather, surveying the estuary brings small return, usual suspects huddled in the lee of any rise in ground, hard to see with buffeting winds and smeared lenses.

Over the breakwater, wind whips surf from waves ridged jade and sandy green under sickly yellow sky. Sand hisses ahead along the beach, heavy boulders seeming weightless above wafting sandy stream-lines: *Oystercatchers* beat over the sea, cries faint in roar of wind and surf; *Turnstones* speed low and *Redshank* rocket along the shore. A tight flock of fifty *Knot* lift from rocks, grey and sharp-winged, prospecting the strand in tight formation before passing high overhead. A *Herring Gull* stands on the bright strand. First diminutive snowy *Sanderlings* of winter huddle close, chasing creamy surf on black legs before taking off as a tight, white flock, fast and low over streaming foam. Four *Mute Swans*, pass majestically high over dunes ahead and out to sea, pure white against black cloud and dark mountains, moving from estuary to sheltered feeding along the coast.

# *Winter Gulls* .................................................................... 13th December

SHARP MORNING WITH BRIGHT SUN, high cloud and a keen south breeze, landscape washed of colour by recent gales and cold. Village and farmland have been quiet for a few weeks now: *Finches*, *Pipits* and *Wagtails* flocked and moved on, only the occasional *Stonechat* and resident *Blackbirds*, *Robins* and *Dunnocks* defending winter territory. *Magpies* mooch about with every black crow species bar *Chough*, foraging throughout farmland, estuary and shore. *Ravens* seem just as happy diving, flip-rolling and soaring over dunes as in mountains.

A straggling row of *Lapwing* oar their way across the landscape, black and white indistinct against low winter sun. With wide, spade-ended wings and easy lope of a flight, they are aptly named: though neither fast nor powerful, they are one of few European species to occasionally make it across the Atlantic against prevailing winds. The ragged line dips low over the estuary, ducking the south wind, streaming along the rocky dyke, wobbling and side-slipping indecisively over emerging green salting before disappearing over the wall.

Wind-whipped wavelets swash over sea-washed turf. Across the brim-full estuary a drift of white gulls stands on emerging salting, roosting, preening or sitting out the high tide, heads to wind. *Herring Gulls* are the standard: white and silver with yellow bills and pink-grey legs. A single *Lesser Black-Backed* stands charcoal-backed with yellow legs amongst the silver; a much larger, pink-grey legged *Great Black-Backed Gull* sits just along the line. Just like smaller, grey-headed *Herring Gulls*, over-wintering *Common Gulls* have greenish legs and lack heavy yellow bill and red spot. Red-legged *Black Headed Gulls* are elegant, tern-like; tails cocked when swimming, black-stained behind the eye. Last week, amongst all the pure white breasts bright in winter sunshine, one was clear roseate pink but refused to meet the other requirements of rare Ross's Gull.

# *Winter Frost* ........................................................... 20th December

DARK MORNING SKIES FADE GREY to pink over frost dry mountains, through gold to thin blue and winter sun; ground like iron; lawns crunchy white all day. *Robins* at first light flit silently almost from underfoot in the lane, not visible until they move. Early *Blackbirds* clatter off in alarm. Late *Tawny Owls* call deep in the woods, one recently in buoyant, broad-winged flight over white fields, black silhouette in greying skies. This morning, the smaller *Woodcock* flew over gorse, broad winged but with greater momentum. The village looks snug, still orange lamp lit, wood-smoke hanging in the wooded valley. *Wood Pigeons* call gently in ivy sprays and a band of *Bullfinches* crosses the lane, 'peeping' quietly to each other.

On the beach, wet sand holds prints well in still, frosty conditions. *Pied Wagtail's* trotting tracks stay clear, even spread of primary feathers imprinted as it flipped up for flies. *Rabbits* use both estuary and shore, distinctive soft-edged oval prints in groups of four reflecting their characteristic lope: forepaws landing first each side, prints between as hind legs catch up. Prints in soft sand are tracked by sets of much smaller, tight groups of four at proportionally much greater spacing: a *Weasel's* inexorable quest for the blood of a selected victim. *Waders* also mark the upper strand, toes wide spread with no hind claw: large printed Curlew with smaller Turnstone and *Ringed Plover*.

Just above the water line, four medium heavy waders stand hunched forward amongst boulders or on wet sand, grey backed on thick set, long legs. Closer views show dark spangled back and short heavy bill, black as the eye. Wings lift high, pale under-wing characteristically marked black, as *Grey Plover* flight out over the waves with plaintive calls, grey and silver with white rump and wing bars.

## *Memorable Images* ............................................. 28th December

WHEN FISHING, 'takes' often come on the first or last cast of perhaps thousands in a day.

Similarly, a memorable image will flash to view before the car is locked or when packing up at the end of a wildlife walk.

Last week, a tight line of fifty *Lapwing* followed the dunes, shifted over the Maes and estuary and passed into the distance, oaring their way in close formation, black and white across hazy grey sky.

Today, agitated *Wagtails* and *Pipits* sounded the alarm as a *Starling* was snatched from the air with a rush of wings and fluttering of hard flight feathers not 10 yards away. A small male *Sparrowhawk* stalled and banked hard down and away, hitting the ground with a soft thud and spread wings before carrying off in heavy flight the now securely gripped, still squawking prey to a quieter spot.

It is worthwhile strolling just further than the access slipway into the boulders to view the end of the bay. A pair of *Shags* find this rocky enough to have stayed for many months; an *Eider* likewise was happy just off shore until the late gales; a *Phalarope* was found swimming in the surf here after storms in early October. Today, a party of *Ringed Plover* briefly lift off and resettle, perfectly marked on new, storm thrown pebbles.

Wildlife will appear mysteriously in the landscape, as did a pair of *Goosander* last week, swimming close off shore in calm water only just carefully scanned: male the colour of sunset on a white wall, dark female sporting a strange brown fringe behind. Unusually, the female was displaying, head and neck outstretched along the water at the male. Later, when packing up the 'scope, the pair were spotted high over the Maes, heading upriver for nest sites.

# English Welsh Taxonomy

TRANSLATION REFERENCES. Birds: *Birds of Merioneth* Peter Hope Jones, Cambrian Ornithological Society, 1974. Plants: *Welsh Names of Plants: Enwau Cymraeg ar Blanhigion* Dafydd Jones as Arthur Jones, National Museum of Wales; Amgueddfa Genedlaethol Cymru, 1995.

## ANIMALS

| | | |
|---:|---|---|
| *ystlumod* | Bat | *Chiroptea sp.* |
| *cocos* | Cockle (Common) | *Cerastoderma edule* |
| *dolffiniaid* | Dolphin | *Delphinidae sp.* |
| *brogaod* | Frog | *Rana temporaria* |
| *morlo llwyd* | Grey Seal | *Halichoerus grypus* |
| *ysgyfarnog* | Hare | *Lepus europaeus* |
| *madfall* | Lizard | *Zootoca vivipara* |
| *minc* | Mink (American) | *Neovison vison* |
| *cregyn gleision* | Mussels | *Mytilus edulis* |
| *dwrgi* | Otter | *Lutra lutra* |
| *ffwlbart* | Polecat | *Mustela putorius* |
| *mochyn mor* | Porpoise (Harbour) | *Phocoena phocoena* |
| *cwningen* | Rabbit | *Oryctolagus cuniculus* |
| *carlwm* | Stoat | *Mustela erminea* |
| *llyffaint* | Toad | *Bufo bufo* |
| *wenci* | Weasel | *Mustela nivalis* |
| *gafr wyllt* | Wild Goat | *Capra aegagrus* |

## BIRDS

| | | |
|---:|---|---|
| *morwennol y gogledd* | Arctic Tern | *Sterna paradisaea* |
| *tylluan wen* | Barn Owl | *Tyto alba* |
| *rhostog gynffonfrith* | Bar-tailed Godwit | *Limosa lipponica* |
| *mwyalchen* | Blackbird | *Turdus merula* |
| *telor penddu* | Blackcap | *Sylvia atricapilla* |
| *gwylan benddu* | Black-Headed Gull | *Laus ridibundus* |
| *titw tomos las* | Blue Tit | *Parus caeruleus* |
| *coch y berllan* | Bullfinch | *Pyrrhula pyrrhula* |
| *bwncath* | Buzzard | *Buteo buteo* |
| *siffsaff* | Chiffchaff | *Phylloscopus collybita* |
| *bran goesgoch* | Chough | *Pyrrhocorax pyrrhocorax* |
| *gwylan y Gweunydd* | Common Gull | *Larus canus* |
| *pibydd y dorlan* | Common Sandpiper | *Tringa hypoleucos* |
| *morwennol gyffredin* | Common Tern | *Sterna hirundo* |
| *mulfran* | Cormorant | *Phalacrocorax carbo* |

| | | |
|---:|---|---|
| *bran* | Corvid | *Corvus sp.* |
| *gylfinir* | Curlew | *Numeneus arquata* |
| *pibydd cambig* | Curlew Sandpiper | *Calidris ferruginea* |
| *bronwen-y-dwr* | Dipper | *Cinclus cinclus* |
| *trochydd* | Diver | *Gavia sp.* |
| *pibydd y mawn* | Dunlin | *Calidris alpina* |
| *llwyd y gwrych* | Dunnock | *Prunella modularis* |
| *hwyaden fwythblu* | Eider | *Somateria mollissima* |
| *socan eira* | Fieldfare | *Turdus pilaris* |
| *aderyn-drycin y graig* | Fulmar | *Fulmarus glacialis* |
| *hugan* | Gannet | *Sula bassana* |
| *telor yr ardd* | Garden Warbler | *Sylvia borin* |
| *rhostog* | Godwit | *Limosa sp.* |
| *dryw eurben* | Goldcrest | *Regulus regulus* |
| *hwyden lygad-aur* | Goldeneye | *Bucephala clangula* |
| *nico* | Goldfinch | *Carduelis carduelis* |
| *hwyden ddanheddog* | Goosander | *Mergus merganser* |
| *troellwr bach* | Grasshopper Warbler | *Locustella naevia* |
| *gwylan gefnddu fwyaf* | Great Black-Backed Gull | *Larus marinus* |
| *titw mawr* | Great Tit | *Parus major* |
| *cnocell werdd* | Green Woodpecker | *Picus viridis* |
| *llinos werdd* | Greenfinch | *Carduelis chloris* |
| *pibydd goeswerdd* | Greenshank | *Tringa nebularia* |
| *creyr glas* | Grey Heron | *Ardea cinerea* |
| *llydandroed llwyd* | Grey Phalarope | *Phalaropus fulicarius* |
| *cwtiad llwyd* | Grey Plover | *Pluvialis squatarola* |
| *siglen lwyd* | Grey Wagtail | *Motacilla cinerea* |
| *gwyach gopog* | Gt Crested Grebe | *Podiceps cristatus* |
| *cnocell fraith fwyaf* | Gt Spotted Woodpecker | *Dendrocopos major* |
| *gwylog* | Guillemot | *Uria aalge* |
| *gwylan y penwaig* | Herring Gull | *Larus argentatus* |
| *gwennol y bondo* | House Martin | *Delichon urbica* |
| *giach fach* | Jack Snipe | *Limnocryptes minimus* |
| *jac-y-do* | Jackdaw | *Corvus monedula* |
| *ysgrech y coed* | Jay | *Garrulus glandarius* |
| *cudyll coch* | Kestrel | *Falco tinnunculus* |
| *gwylan goesddu* | Kittiwakes | *Rissa tridactyla* |
| *pibydd yr aber* | Knot | *Calidris canutus* |

| | | |
|---|---|---|
| *cornchwiglen* | Lapwing | *Vanellus vanellus* |
| *gwylan gefnddu leiaf* | Lesser Black-Backed Gull | *Larus fuscus* |
| *llinos* | Linnet | *Acanthis cannabina* |
| *creyr bach* | Little Egret | *Egretta garzetta* |
| *gwyach fach* | Little Grebe | *Tachybaptus ruficollis* |
| *gwylan fechan* | Little Gull | *Larus minutus* |
| *morwennol fechan* | Little Tern | *Sterna albifrons* |
| *titw gynffon hir* | Long Tailed Tit | *Aegithalos caudatus* |
| *pioden* | Magpie | *Pica pica* |
| *hwyaden wyllt* | Mallard | *Anas platyrhincos* |
| *aderyn-drycin manaw* | Manx Shearwater | *Puffinus puffinus* |
| *corhedydd y waun* | Meadow Pipit | *Anthus pratensis* |
| *hwyaden frongoch* | Merganser | *Mergus serrator* |
| *cudyll bach* | Merlin | *Falco columbarius* |
| *alarch dof* | Mute Swan | *Cygnus olor* |
| *troellwr* | Nightjars | *Caprimulgus europaeus* |
| *pioden y mor* | Oystercatcher | *Haematopus ostralegus* |
| *hebog tramor* | Peregrine | *Falco peregrinus* |
| *gwybedog brith* | Pied Flycatcher | *Muscicapa striata* |
| *siglen fraith* | Pied Wagtail | *Motacilla alba* |
| *hwyaden lostfain* | Pintail | *Anas acuta* |
| *pal* | Puffin | *Fratercula arctica* |
| *cigfran* | Raven | *Corvus corax* |
| *llur* | Razorbills | *Alca torda* |
| *barcud coch* | Red Kite | *Milvus milvus* |
| *trochydd gyddfgoch* | Red Throated Divers | *Gavia stellata* |
| *llinos bengoch* | Redpoll | *Acanthis flammea* |
| *pibydd goesgoch* | Redshank | *Tringa totanus* |
| *tingoch* | Redstart | *Phoenicurus phoenicurus* |
| *coch dan-aden* | Redwing | *Turdus iliacus* |
| *bras y cyrs* | Reed Bunting | *Emberiza schoeniclus* |
| *telor y cyrs* | Reed Warbler | *Aquacephalus scirpaceus* |
| *mwyalchen y mynedd* | Ring Ouzel | *Turdus torquatus* |
| *cwtiad torchog* | Ringed Plover | *Charadrius hiaticula* |
| *robin goch* | Robin | *Erithacus rubecula* |
| *gwennol y glenydd* | Sand Martin | *Riparia riparia* |
| *pibydd y tywod* | Sanderling | *Calidris alba* |
| *morwennol bigddu* | Sandwich Terns | *Sternus sandvicensis* |

| | | |
|---:|---|---|
| *mor-hwyaden ddu* | Scoter | *Melanitta nigra* |
| *telor y hesg* | Sedge Warbler | *Acrocephalus schoenobinus* |
| *mulfran werdd* | Shag | *Phalocrocorax aristotelis* |
| *aderyn-drycin* | Shearwaters | *Puffinus sp.* |
| *hwyaden yr eithin* | Shelduck | *Tadorna tadorna* |
| *pila gwyrdd* | Siskin | *Carduelis spinus* |
| *ehedydd* | Skylark | *Alauda arvensis* |
| *giach gyffredin* | Snipe | *Gallinago gallinago* |
| *bronfraith* | Song Thrush | *Turdus philomelos* |
| *gwalch glas* | Sparrowhawk | *Accipiter nisus* |
| *drudwen* | Starling | *Sturnus vulgaris* |
| *clochdar y cerrig* | Stonechat | *Saxicola torquata* |
| *gwennol* | Swallow | *Hirundo rustica* |
| *gwennol ddu* | Swift | *Apus apus* |
| *tylluan frech* | Tawny Owl | *Strix aluco* |
| *corhwyaden* | Teal | *Anas crecca* |
| *cwtiad y traeth* | Turnstones | *Arenaria interpres* |
| *siglen* | Wagtails | *Motacilla sp.* |
| *tinwen y garn* | Wheatear | *Oenanthe oenanthe* |
| *coeggylfinir* | Whimbrel | *Numenius phaeopus* |
| *siglen wen* | White Wagtail | *Motacilla alba alba* |
| *llwyd fron* | Whitethroat | *Sylvia communis* |
| *chwiwell* | Wigeon | *Anas penelope* |
| *telor y helyg* | Willow Warbler | *Phylloscopus trochilus* |
| *ysguthan* | Wood Pigeon | *Columba palumbus* |
| *cyffylog* | Woodcock | *Scolopax rusticola* |
| *dryw* | Wren | *Troglodytes troglodytes* |
| *siglen felen* | Yellow Wagtail | *Motacilla flava* |
| *melyn y eithin* | Yellowhammer | *Emberiza citrinella* |

## FISH

| | | |
|---:|---|---|
| *bas* | Bass | *Micropterus salmoides* |
| *llygad maharen* | Blenny | *Lipophrys pholis* |
| *brithyll* | Brown Trout | *Salmo trutta* |
| *penllwyd* | Grayling | *Thymallus thymallus* |
| *hyrddyn* | Mullet Grey | *Mugil cephalus* |

| | | |
|---:|:---|:---|
| *eog* | Salmon | *Salmo salar* |
| *llyswennod tywod* | Sand Eel | *Hyperoplus sp.* |
| *goby* | Sand Goby | *Pomatoschistus minitus* |
| *sewin* | Sea Trout | *Salmo trutta* |

## INSECTS

| | | |
|---:|:---|:---|
| *coch y bonddu* | Garden Chafers | *Phyllopertha horticola* |
| *'harddwch derw gwyfynod'* | Oak Beauty Moth | *Biston strataria* |

## PLANTS (incl. FUNGI)

| | | |
|---:|:---|:---|
| *acacia* | Acacia | *Acacia* |
| *gwernen* | Alder | *Alnus glutinosa* |
| *pren afalau* | Apple | *Malus domestica* |
| *onnen* | Ash | *Fraxinus excelsior* |
| *tegeirian y gwenyn* | Bee Orchid | *Ophrys apifera* |
| *ffawydden gopr* | Beech, Copper | *Fagus sylvatica* Atropurpurea Group |
| *bedwen arian* | Birch | *Betula pendula* |
| *berwr* | Bittercress | *Cardamine sp.* |
| *draenen ddu* | Blackthorn | *Prunus spinosa* |
| *bladderwrack* | Bladderwrack | *Fuscus vesiculus* |
| *clychau'r gog* | Bluebell | *Hyacinthoides non-scripta* |
| *rhedynen gyffredin* | Bracken | *Pteridium aquilinem* |
| *mwyaren ddu* | Bramble | *Rubus fruticosus* |
| *gwinwydden ddu* | Bryony | *Tamus communis* |
| *bwdleia* | Buddleia | *Buddleia sp.* |
| *rhosyn draenllwyn* | Burnet Rose | *Rosa pimpinellafolia* |
| *tafod y gors* | Butterwort | *Pinguicula vulgaris* |
| *cedrwydd* | Cedar, Atlantic | *Cedrus atlantica* |
| *llygad ebrill* | Celandine | *Ranunculus ficaria* |
| *gaugeiriosen* | Cherry Plum | *Prunus cerasifera* |
| *llysiau'r oen* | Corn Salad | *Valeriana locusta* |

| | | |
|---|---|---|
| *cwyros* | Cornelian Cherry | *Cornus mas* |
| *pren afal sur* | Crab Apple | *Malus sylvestris* |
| *corhelygen* | Creeping Willow | *Salix repens* |
| *bara'r hwch* | Cyclamen | *Cyclamen hederifolium* |
| *llygad y dydd* | Daisy | *Bellis perennis* |
| *eirin duon* | Damson | *Prunus domestica subsp. Insititia* |
| *dant y llew* | Dandelion | *Taraxicum officinale* |
| *mwyaren fair* | Dewberry | *Rubus caesius* |
| *rhosyn coch gwyllt* | Dog-rose | *Rosa canina* |
| *trilliw y tywyn* | Dune Pansy | *Viola tricolor subsp. curtisii* |
| *melyn yr hwyr* | Evening Primrose | *Oenothera biennis* |
| *effros* | Eyebright | *Euphrasia sp.* |
| *llin y tylwith teg* | Fairy Flax | *Linum cathartica* |
| *forsythia* | Forsythia | *Forsythis sp.* |
| *byssed y cwn* | Foxgloves | *Digitalis purpurea* |
| *sampier y geifr* | Golden (Rock) Samphire | *Inula crithnoides* |
| *serenllys mawr* | Greater Stitchwort | *Stellaria holostea* |
| *draenen wen* | Hawthorn | *Crataegus monogyna* |
| *collen* | Hazel | *Corylus avellana* |
| *marchrawn* | Horsetails | *Equisetum ps.* |
| *iorwg* | Ivy | *Hedera helix* |
| *llin y fagwyr* | Ivy-leaved Toadflax | *Cymbalaria muralis* |
| *briwydden felen* | Ladies' Bedstraw | *Galium verum* |
| *llarwydd* | Larch | *Larix sp.* |
| *lavwr* | Laver | *Porphyra umbilicalis* |
| *penigan gwfaidyry* | Maiden Pink | *Dianthus deltoides* |
| *moresg* | Marram | *Ammophila arenaria* |
| *caldrist y gors* | Marsh Helleborine | *Epipactis palustris* |
| *llyrlys* | Marsh Samphire | *Salicornia europaea* |
| *pannog* | Mullein | *Verbascum sp.* |
| *madarchen* | Mushrooms | *Agaricus sp.* |
| *derwen* | Oak | *Quercus sp.* |
| *gellygen* | Pear | *Pyrus sp.* |
| *cneuen ddaear* | Pignut | *Conopodium majus* |
| *llwynhidydd* | Plantain | *Plantago sp.* |
| *dyfrillys* | Pondweed | *Potamogeton sp.* |
| *briallu* | Primrose | *Primula vulgaris* |

| | | |
|---|---|---|
| *tegeirian era* | Pyramidal Orchid | *Anacamptis pyramidalis* |
| *craf y geifr* | Ramsons | *Allium ursinum* |
| *gludlys goch* | Red Campion | *Silene dioica* |
| *meillionen goch* | Red Clover | *Trifolium pratense* |
| *tagaradr* | Restharrow | *Ononis sp.* |
| *corn carw'r mawr* | Rock Samphire | *Crithmum maritimum* |
| *cerddinen* | Rowan | *Sorbus aucuparia* |
| *helygen grynddial fwyaf* | Sallow (Goat Willow) | *Salix caprea* |
| *llyrlys* | Samphire | *Salicornica sp.* |
| *craf nadroedd* | Sand Leek | *Allium scorodoprasum* |
| *taglys arfor* | Sea Bindweed | *Calystegia soldanella* |
| *celyn y mor* | Sea Holly | *Eryngium maritimum* |
| *craith unnos* | Self Heal | *Prunella vulgaris* |
| *clefryn* | Sheeps Bit | *Jasione montana* |
| *suran* | Sorrel | *Rumex sp.* |
| *rhywyddlwyn* | Speedwell | *Veronica sp.* |
| *serenllys* | Stitchwort | *Stellaria* |
| *gwithlys* | Sundew | *Drosera sp.* |
| *masarnen* | Sycamore | *Acer pseudoplatanus* |
| *gruw gwyllt* | Thyme | *Thymus sp.* |
| *hocyswydden* | Tree Mallow | *Lavatera arborea* |
| *pysen y ceirw* | Trefoil | *Trifolium sp.* |
| *ffugbysen* | Vetch | *Vicia sp.* |
| *fioled bêr* | Violet, Sweet | *Viola odorata* |
| *crafanc y dwr* | Water Crowfoot | *Ranunculus aquatilis* |
| *helygen* | Willow | *Salix sp.* |
| *gwlydden Rhudd* | Winter Purslane | *Claytonia sibirica* |
| *blodyn y gwynt* | Wood Anemone | *Anemone nemorosa* |
| *suran y coed* | Wood Sorrel | *Oxalis acetosella* |
| *briwydden ber* | Woodruff | *Galium odoratum* |
| *crebell felen* | Yellow Rattle | *Rhinanthus minor* |